SWEENEY TODD
THE BARBER

a melodrama in four acts

adapted by

BRIAN J. BURTON

from George Dibdin Pitt's Victorian version

of the legendary drama

MUSIC AND LYRICS BY

BRIAN J. BURTON

COMBRIDGE JACKSON LIMITED

BAYLISS HOUSE · HURST STREET · BIRMINGHAM B5 4BT

First published 1962
by C. COMBRIDGE LTD.,

BIRMINGHAM

1964, 1965, 1966, 1967, 1969, 1970, 1971, 1973, 1976

INTRODUCTION

The legend which provides the story for this melodrama dates back to fourteenth century France when a certain barber on the Ile de Cité was reputed to have cut throats and disposed of his victims in a highly unconventional manner.

During the first three or four decades of the nineteenth century there was a revival of interest in things horrific and the old story was 'dusted off' and reappeared with its setting changed to late eighteenth century London. It was published as a serial in a series of sixpenny novels called *The People's Periodical and Family Library* under the title 'The String of Pearls' or 'The Sailor's Gift'.

It was this nineteenth century 'horror comic' that George Dibdin Pitt used as the basis of his play 'The String of Pearls' or 'The Fiend of Fleet Street'. Although this was set in the time of George II, the style was unmistakably that which we now associate with early Victorian melodrama and so it was decided to place this new version in the early Victorian period.

The original play contained a number of anomalies and anachronisms and the decision to advance the period created even more but as those in the original were quite amusing no attempt has been made to correct them.

This new version follows very closely that of Pitt but whereas his was little longer than a 'curtain raiser', this has been expanded into a full-length play. A number of songs in the Victorian manner have been written by the present adapter and included in the play. This is no innovation as records show that most melodramas of the period included sentimental ballads and comedy songs. The former were often sung by a female infant prodigy of the time who played the part of a boy. In keeping with this tradition the role of Tobias in this version has been written for a girl.

The photographs in this book are from the production at the Crescent Theatre where this version was first presented.

THE ACTION OF THE PLAY TAKES PLACE IN LONDON IN THE 1840's

ACT ONE:	*Scene One:*	Fleet Street, outside Sweeney Todd's shop.
	Scene Two:	Interior of Sweeney Todd's shop.
	Scene Three:	Breakfast parlour in the house of Jasper Oakley.
ACT TWO:	*Scene One:*	The parlour behind Mrs Lovett's pie shop in Bell Yard.
	Scene Two:	Interior of Sweeney Todd's shop.
	Scene Three:	Interior of Mrs Lovett's pie shop.
	Scene Four:	The bakehouse.
ACT THREE:	*Scene One:*	Interior of Sweeney Todd's shop.
	Scene Two:	A chamber in the madhouse.
	Scene Three:	Temple Stairs.
	Scene Four:	A court of Justice.
ACT FOUR:	*Scene One:*	The entrance to Newgate Prison.
	Scene Two:	The bakehouse.
	Scene Three:	Temple Stairs.
	Scene Four:	Sweeney Todd's shop.

The running time of this version (including the songs) is two hours fifteen minutes (excluding intervals).
The play was presented at the Crescent Theatre in one basic set (the barber's shop) and a number of inserts and dropcloths. (See illustrations facing page 33). By using traverse curtains for alternate scenes the time taken to effect a change is only a matter of a few seconds.

CHARACTERS IN THE PLAY

SWEENEY TODD—*the barber of Fleet Street*
EZEKIEL SMITH—*a mechanic*
MRS RAGG—*a poor woman*
TOBIAS RAGG—*her son, an apprentice boy*
MARK INGESTRE—*a mariner*
JEAN PARMINE—*a lapidary*
JOHANNA OAKLEY—*a young lady in love*
COLONEL EUSTACE JEFFREY—*of the Indian Army*
JASPER OAKLEY—*a spectacle maker*
MRS OAKLEY—*his wife*
DR AMINADAB LUPIN—*a wolf in sheep's clothing*
MRS LOVETT—*Todd's accomplice in guilt*
JARVIS WILLIAMS—*a lad with an appetite*
JONAS FOGG—*the keeper of the madhouse*
SIR WILLIAM BRANDON—*a judge*
MRS POORLEAN—*an unfortunate woman*

A court usher, two warders, a keeper, three bystanders. By doubling certain parts this play can be presented with seven men and seven women.

TO FRANK JONES

SWEENEY TODD THE BARBER was first presented at the Crescent Theatre, Birmingham, on 16th June, 1962, with the following cast:

Sweeney Todd.....................Frank Jones
Ezekiel Smith.................Charles Cruxton
Mrs Ragg........................Anjela Colley
Tobias Ragg....................Sheila Corbett
Mark Ingestre.................Ronald Barber
Jean Parmine..................Gordon Jackson
Johanna Oakley...............Jennifer Hubner
Colonel Eustace Jeffrey........Michael Booth
Jasper Oakley.....................Fred Smith
Mrs Oakley...................Audrey Waterson
Dr Aminadab Lupin................Ron Sadler
Mrs Lovett.....................Frances Bull
Jarvis Williams..............Michael McGrath
Jonas Fogg......................Bert Briscoe
Sir William Brandon..........Bernard Brunner
Mrs Poorlean....................Anjela Colley

Other parts played by:

Dan Cockburn, Ann Dixon, Patricia Harrison, Margaret Hunt, Geraldine Johnson, Davina Lees, Eddy Lowe, Pauline Smith and Gordon Steff.

The play was directed by John Taylor and Brian J. Burton
with settings designed by Eric Laight
and costumes by Pamela Bishton
Lighting by Richard Palmer
The photographs are by Lisel Haas

ACT ONE

SCENE ONE

FLEET STREET. *When the curtain rises the stage is in darkness. A nearby clock is striking the hour of nine. As it strikes, the lights on stage right come up slowly to reveal part of the graveyard of St Dunstan's Church. On the last stroke the rest of the stage lighting comes up to show the exterior of the barber's shop of Sweeney Todd on the left side of the stage.* SWEENEY TODD *is standing by the shop door. He is in conversation with* EZEKIEL SMITH, *a mechanic.*

Todd : So, Mr Smith, if I have comprehended your mission correctly, you are come on the matter of that little consideration you would have me believe to be owing to you in respect of your mechanical toy.
Smith : Yes, Mr Todd, that is so. I have brought the account with me; I have it here. (*He produces a document from his pocket*). I will read it to you. 'Account owing to Mr Ezekiel Smith in respect of . . . '
Todd : I am fully aware of the details, Mr Smith. Just state the amount of money you are attempting to rob me of.
Smith : No robbery, Mr Todd, only my just reward for labour.
Todd : The amount, fool, the amount!
Smith : Well then, Mr Todd, as to the amount—that is seven pounds eighteen shillings and ninepence halfpenny.
Todd : And ninepence halfpenny ?
Smith : Yes, Mr Todd.
Todd : And what may the ninepence halfpenny be for, Mr Smith ?
Smith : For one pound of ten inch nails, Mr Todd.
Todd : And has it perhaps occurred to you, Mr Smith, that there are some parties that might consider ninepence halfpenny a little excessive for a pound of ten inch nails ?
Smith : It has occurred to me that I do not like your manner of haggling, Mr Todd. Do you be pleased to pay me this minute and let me go.

Todd: Come a little nearer, Mr Smith—just a little nearer if you please. (SMITH *approaches* TODD *with great caution*). That's better, Mr Smith—much better—now we can talk together in a more friendly manner, can we not?
Smith: If you say so, Mr Todd.
Todd: Now then, what would you say to a guinea and a half, Mr Smith, eh—eh? (*leaning towards him*) and perhaps a free shave too—afterwards?
Smith: I'll tell you what I'd say, Mr Todd.
Todd: Yes, Mr Smith?
Smith: I'd say that you are a rogue, Mr Todd, a rogue!
Todd (*aside*): This individual annoys me. I dislike his method of grabbing money, I dislike it very much. In fact my gorge rises. I think him mean. With all the pleasure in the world I would shave him, shave him close, shave him very close indeed. (*Aloud*) I tell you what I'll do, Mr Smith, I'll be fair with us both. I will make it thirty shillings, Mr Smith. A mere matter of one and sixpence will scarcely embarrass an individual in such a prosperous way of business as yourself. Come now, Mr Smith, let us say thirty shillings.
Smith (*earnestly*): Has it occurred to you that there are certain parties not very far up this street—certain legal parties as you might phrase it—who might gain a good deal of profit and instruction from a perusal of some of the items and specifications in this little account of mine?
Todd: And what are you intending to infer by those remarks, Mr Smith?
Smith: Let me finish, Mr Todd, let me finish. The best and most interesting part is yet to be told. I known of a place, that perhaps we might call a school, that is a little higher up this very street where there are a number of individuals who keep little bills like this one for their school books. Do you know to where I refer, Mr Todd?
Todd: I neither know nor care one jot. I am of the opinion that you are out of your mind, Mr Smith—out of your mind.
Smith: I was never saner, Mr Todd. You know full well the place I have in mind—the Old Bailey, Mr Todd—the Old Bailey! (*Aside*) That will quieten him, I think. (*Aloud*)

I believe the amount we mentioned was seven, eighteen, nine and a half, Mr Todd.

Todd : I was speaking about a free shave, Mr Smith. (*Brandishing his razor under* SMITH's *throat*). Now that I look at you closely I discern a certain roughness about the region of your lower lip and a hairiness about your throat that makes my razor long to be at it. Pray, Mr Smith, come inside this minute and I'll attend to you in no time at all. Come now, Mr Smith, and take a seat inside my shop. It will give me the greatest pleasure in the world to polish you off. (*He pushes* SMITH *into the shop, closes the door on him and returns centre stage to sing*) :

"SWEENEY TODD THE BARBER"

(SWEENEY TODD)

I'm Sweeney Todd the barber
And wicked thoughts I harbour.
When I've got him in my chair
I'll do more than cut his hair.
He'll find out and to his cost,
All he owned in life is lost.
Ho! Ho! Ho! I'll polish him off.
Ho! Ho! Ho! I'll polish him off.
He's got a 'luvely' throat for a razor.
Ho! Ho! Ho! I'll polish him off.

I'm Sweeney Todd the barber
And wicked thoughts I harbour.
He'll wait for me to begin
To operate upon his chin.
But indeed that's not my will.
Shaving doesn't pay the bill.
No! No! No! I polish 'em off.
No! No! No! I polish 'em off.
They've got such 'luvely' throats for a razor.
So! So! So! I polish 'em off.

I'm Sweeney Todd the barber
And wicked thoughts I harbour.

When I raise my brush and comb
He will wish he'd stayed at home.
When he thinks that I'm but starting,
I will expedite his 'parting'.
Ho! Ho! Ho! I'll polish him off.
Ho! Ho! Ho! I'll polish him off.
He's got a 'luvely' throat for a razor.
Ho! Ho! Ho! I'll polish him off.

Todd : Ha! If my eyes don't deceive me, I believe I see Mrs Ragg coming here.

SMITH *opens the door of the shop and emerges with caution.* TODD *sees him and pouncing on him, takes him downstage left.*

Todd : Now just you wait a moment or two, Mr Smith, and I'll be free to seal our little bargain—eh ? (*Calling off*). Good morning to you, Mrs Ragg. Come along now, come along, this way. (*Moves to centre stage to meet her*).

MRS RAGG *enters right followed by her son* TOBIAS. *He is a young boy about twelve years old.* (*It is intended that this part be played by a girl*).

Mrs Ragg : Good morning to you, Mr Todd.

Todd : I see you have brought me the little whelp.

Mrs Ragg : 'E ain't a little whelp, Mr Todd, and I won't 'ave you call 'im so—that I won't, Mr Todd.

Todd : Only my fun, Mrs Ragg, only my fun. You know that I dearly love a jest.

Mrs Ragg : That is as may be, Mr Todd. All I know is that I 'ave brought you my boy, Tobias, to be your apprentice as you 'ave said you would 'ave 'im as such and 'ere 'e is. And 'e ain't no whelp that 'e ain't. And what is more, Mr Todd, I 'ave you to remember that 'e is very 'dellikite' and not to work 'im too 'ard. 'E comes of a very 'dellikite' family 'e does and is very easily upset. Ain't you my little lamb ?

Tobias : Oh yes please, Ma.

Mrs Ragg : And I axe you to remember likewise, Mr Todd, that my little Tobias 'as been tenderly nurtured and to treat 'im as such.

Todd : That goes without the necessity of saying, Mrs Ragg.

I doubt if you would find a kinder more considerate employer in the length and breadth of London, let alone here in Fleet Street. I will treat your boy Tobias as I would my own son, my own flesh and blood, Mrs Ragg. I love boys and treat them the way they deserve you may be sure. So go along now, Mrs Ragg, and have no fears about this dear little lad, none at all.

Mrs Ragg: As you say sir. With which I says good morning and leaves you to 'im, Mr Todd.

Todd (*to* TOBIAS, *watching* MRS RAGG *as she goes out*): Come along, come along my young friend. (*Exit* MRS RAGG).

Todd (*grabbing* TOBIAS *and dragging him down right*): Now remember this, Tobias Ragg, remember it well. You are my apprentice and that you have had of me board, lodging and washing—you understand boy?

Tobias: Yes sir.

Todd: Save that you will take your meals at home, that you don't sleep here and that your mother gets up your linen. (*Fiercely*) Now are you not a fortunate, happy dog? (TOBIAS *doesn't answer but cowers timidly*). Well answer me lad, answer me!

Tobias: Yes sir.

Todd: Yes sir, what sir? What are you boy?

Tobias: What sir?

Todd: Answer me—what—are—you? (*Shaking* TOBIAS).

Tobias: I'm . . . a happy fortunate dog, Mr Todd.

Todd (*standing back and smiling*): That's better boy, much better. I can see that you and I will get on very well, Tobias —very well indeed. I like you, Tobias, you're a nice boy. (*Leaning towards* TOBIAS, *fiercely*) But I'll cut your throat from ear to ear if you repeat one word, just one word mind you, of what passes in this shop, or if you dare to make any supposition, or draw any conclusion from anything you may see or hear. Do you understand me, Tobias?

Tobias: Oh, Mr Todd!

Todd: Not 'Oh, Mr Todd,' but 'No, Mr Todd,' boy. 'No, I won't say a word.' Do—you—understand? (*The words are punctuated by punches on the head*).

Tobias: Yes, Mr Todd. I won't say anything, Mr Todd, I

swear it. If I do may I—may I be made into veal pies at Lovett's in Bell Yard.

Todd : What was that you said—boy—eh ? (*Takes his ear*).

Tobias : Veal pies, Mr Todd.

Todd : How dare you mention veal pies in my presence ? (*Aside*) Does he suspect ? (*Aloud*) Tell me boy do you suspect ?

Tobias : Oh sir, I don't suspect—indeed I don't. I meant no harm in making the remark.

Todd (*eyeing* TOBIAS *narrowly*) : Very good. I'm satisfied—quite satisfied! And, mark me, the shop, and the shop only, is your place.

Tobias : Yes sir.

Todd : And if any customer gives you a penny, you can keep it, my boy, you can keep it.

Tobias : Thank you kindly, Mr Todd.

Todd : And when you get enough pennies, Tobias, then you'll be a rich man won't you ?

Tobias : Yes sir, you're very kind.

Todd : Good, but I'll be even kinder. I'll tell you what I'll do for you boy. I'll take care of the pennies for you and when I think you require any I'll consider whether—(*Aside*) But who's this ? His dress and manner bespeak him a seafaring man and a stranger in these parts.

MARK INGESTRE *enters right. He is dressed as a sea captain. He walks across the stage examining the names above the shops.* TOBIAS *sees him and goes across and talks to him.* TODD *goes down left to* SMITH.

Todd : I fancy, Mr Mechanic, that I have business with this gentleman. If you will call again some time next week we may find time to discuss that little matter you mentioned earlier. Thirty shillings, I think you said, was the sum mentioned between us. In the meantime I dare swear that you have a great deal of business on hand in other parts of the city. I wish you good morning. (*Returns to shop door*).

Smith : I will go now, but I will be back earlier than next week, Mr Todd. (*Aside*) Oh yes—much earlier than next week. (*Exit* SMITH).

TODD *watches* TOBIAS *from the shop door.*

Mark (*to* TOBIAS) : I thank you my good boy for the information you have so kindly afforded me. You say that you know Miss Johanna Oakley ?

Tobias : Yes sir, I am acquainted with Miss Johanna. She is a kind-hearted lady. Shortly after my father's death sickness and sorrow overcame my poor mother and myself. Had it not been for Miss Oakley's timely aid, both of us might have perished for want.

Mark (*aside as he moves away left*) : How it gladdens a person's heart to hear his sweetheart so highly esteemed. (*Aloud—turning towards* TOBIAS) Miss Johanna Oakley is my affianced bride. For five years have I been absent from the country that gave me birth and from the home I love so well. My vessel unexpectedly arrived at this port this morning and no sooner did I place foot on shore but I naturally felt a desire to seek out my old friends. Judge of my mortification and surprise when I was told that they were not known at their former address, but had removed, no one knew whither. Heaven alone knows how I should have discovered them had it not been for the valuable information with which you have supplied me.

Tobias : How I should love to become a sailor! Happy and joyous in my freedom, breathing the fresh pure air of liberty!

TOBIAS *moves centre stage to sing* :

SAILING AWAY (TOBIAS)

REFRAIN I

Sailing away, sailing way over the sea.
Sailing away, joyous and happy and free.
White clouds above floating along in the blue.
Free as the air, no need for care,
Sailing way over the sea.

VERSE I

It is so gloomy in London Town,
When the grey fog comes stealing down.
Ships on the river draw me their way.
Oh, how I hope that one fine day—I'll be :-

REFRAIN II

Sailing away, sailing way over the sea.
Sailing away, joyous and happy and free.
White clouds above floating along in the blue.
Free as the air, no need for care,
Sailing way over the sea.

VERSE II

I cannot really believe that I,
Always will live under this dull sky.
If I work hard and save my pay
Ere very long I'll be on my way.

REFRAIN III

Sailing away, sailing way over the sea.
Sailing away, joyous and happy and free.
White clouds above floating along in the blue.
This is my plan, ere I'm a man,
I'll be way over the sea.

Mark: The sea has its perils and its chances. I have been captain of the good ship *Star* for five years. During that time I have saved ten thousand pounds, besides being the possessor of a string of pearls . . .

Chords of music.

Todd (*moving down left to make his aside*): A string of pearls!

Mark: . . . worth twelve thousand more.

Todd (*moving across to* TOBIAS): Ah, Toby, my dear—what a time you have been. What has detained you my darling boy?

Tobias (*backing in fear*): Sir, Mr Todd, sir, I . . .

Todd (*with saccharin sweetness*): Has Captain Pearson's wig been sent home my dear?

Tobias: I—I—I don't know sir, Mr Todd.

Todd (*closing on* TOBIAS—*fiercely*): I thought I gave you strict instructions not to speak to any person when out of my sight—eh—eh?

Tobias: I don't know sir, you may have done sir—I . . .

Todd (*boxing his ears*): Take that—and remember for the future what it was for. Now, go into the shop and attend to your business—do you hear me—eh?

Tobias: Yes sir, at once sir. (*Runs to shop door*).

Todd: And the next time you disobey me, I'll cut your throat from ear to ear.

TOBIAS *goes into shop.*

Tobias (*putting head round door*): From where to where?

Todd (*going up to* TOBIAS *demonstrating*): From 'ere to 'ere!

Exit TOBIAS.

Mark (*moving to* TODD): Your pardon, sir—I fear I am to blame. I asked him for the address of a particular old friend whom I am most anxious to discover again—we got into conversation—and . . .

Todd: No apologies, I beg. Boys will be boys, and a little mild chastisement from time to time does them no harm.

Mark: Perhaps you are right, but I must protest always against unnecessary severity towards young persons, who can scarcely be expected to answer for every little fault when hardly capable of judging which is right and wrong. Though hasty, you are no doubt possessed of a generous heart, and hang me if I don't patronise you this very moment. I am going to meet my sweetheart presently, and I think a clean face will become so important an occasion.

TOBIAS *puts head round door of shop to listen.*

Todd: I am happy to be of service to you good gentleman. Is it a shave you need? What am I here for but to give you a shave (*leaning towards* MARK)—to give you a closer shave than you ever had before?

Tobias (*signalling to* MARK *behind* TODD'S *back*): You mustn't go in—don't go, don't go, please sir!

Todd (*turning swiftly to* TOBIAS): By the way, Tobias, while I am—'operating'—on this gentleman's—chin—the figures of St Dunstan's clock are about to strike—the exhibition will excite your curiosity and allow me time to shave our customer without interruption. (*Pushes* TOBIAS *down right*).

Tobias: Please, Mr Todd, can't I . . .

Todd: Cannot you what boy?

Tobias: Can't I stay and lather him?

Todd (*fiercely*): Get out, I tell you, GET OUT!

Exit TOBIAS *running.*

Todd (*to* MARK *after a short pause*) : I am like a father to that darling boy, sir. I love him—positively dote on him, (*aside*) so much so that I feel I could polish him off. (*Aloud*) Dear me, I had quite forgotten that you are perhaps in a hurry sir. This way if you please sir—pray come in sir.

TODD *opens the door of the shop and ushers* MARK *in. He follows and closes the door but opens it again at once, puts his head round it and sings :*

SWEENEY TODD THE BARBER (reprise)
(SWEENEY TODD)

I'm Sweeney Todd the barber,
And wicked thoughts I harbour.
He believes I'll comb his quiff,
But in less than half a jiff,
I am such a dreadful feller,
I'll tip this 'salt' into my cellar.
Ho! Ho! Ho! I'll polish him off.
Ho! Ho! Ho! I'll polish him off.
He's got a 'luvely' throat for a razor.
Ho! Ho! Ho! I'll polish him off.

He withdraws into the shop and closes the door quickly.
The stage lighting begins to fade except for that covering the churchyard area. As it does so the church clock begins to strike and SMITH *returns from stage right and tiptoes over to a gravestone.*

Smith (*shaking his fist at the shop door*) : I have come back, Mr Todd, as I told you I would. And much earlier than next week. Oh yes, Mr Todd, very much earlier!

He touches a secret spring and the gravestone opens like a door and he disappears through it as the lights fade to blackout.

CURTAIN

ACT ONE

SCENE TWO

SWEENEY TODD'S SHOP. *There is an entrance down right and another up right. A barber's chair is set upstage centre with a cupboard to the left of it. On top of the cupboard are the various items of barber's equipment including shaving mugs, brushes, combs, razors, etc. Slightly downstage of the main chair, and to its left and right are two other chairs. These are smaller, however, and can be moved around the stage as required. There are a number of shelves and cupboards on the back wall on which can be seen bottles of lotion, wigs and so on.*

MARK *enters from down right followed by* TODD.

Todd: Will you be pleased to seat yourself (*pointing to centre chair*). This chair I think you will find the most comfortable, sir.

MARK *sits* — TODD *takes up his position by chair and starts to brush* MARK'S *hair.*

Todd: Just turn your head a little on one side, that's it sir, that will do. You've been to sea sir? (*Crosses to cupboard for a towel*).

Mark: That I have and but lately have come up the river from an Indian voyage.

Todd: You carry some treasures I presume?

Mark: Indeed yes, among others this small casket. (*He produces it from his pocket*).

Todd (*crossing to examine it*): Ah—a piece of exquisite workmanship.

Mark: It is not the box but the contents that must cause you wonder, for I must, in confidence, tell you it contains a string of veritable pearls of the value of twelve thousand pounds.

Music.

Todd (*aside—chuckling and whetting razor on palm*): I see that I shall without doubt have to polish him off. (*Aloud*): Ha! ha! ha! Heugh!!!

Mark: What the devil noise was that?

Todd: It was only me—I laughed.

Mark: Laugh! Humph! Do you call that a laugh? It sounds to me as though you caught it of somebody who died. I beg you if that is your manner of laughing not to indulge in it further.

Todd: My humble apologies sir, you will find me all attention to your orders, good sir. (*Puts towel round* MARK'S *neck*). Now sir, I am ready and we can proceed to business if it so please you. It's as well you came here sir, for though I myself say it, there isn't a shaving shop in the length and breadth of the City of London that ever thinks upon polishing off a customer as I do—fact—can assure you—ha! ha! heugh! (*Commences to mix lather*).

Mark: Shiver the main-brace! I tell you, Master Barber, that if you come that laugh again I will get up from this chair and go. I don't like it, I tell you, and there's an end of it.

Todd: Very good—it won't occur again. (*Applying lather to* MARK'S *chin*) If I may be so bold, who are you, where did you come from—and whither are you going?

Mark: Humph!—that's cool, at all events. I thought that... mind what you're doing, you almost had the brush in my mouth. You seem fond of asking questions my friend, very fond. Perhaps before I answer yours you will reply to one I am about to put to you?

Todd: Oh yes, of course, what is it?

Mark: Do you happen to know a Mr Oakley who lives somewhere hereabouts? He is a spectacle maker by trade.

Todd: Yes, to be sure, I know him—Jasper Oakley of Fore Street. He has a daughter called Johanna, whom the young bloods call 'The Flower of Fore Street'. Bless me, where can my strop be? I had it but a minute ago. I must have lain it down somewhere. What an odd thing now that I can't see it. Its very extraordinary what can have become of it. Ah—now I recollect—I took it into my parlour. Sit still, sir; I shan't be a minute. You can amuse yourself with the newspaper.

He crosses in front of MARK. *As he passes him he hands a newspaper to him and goes to the door up right. He turns before going out—*

Todd (*aside*) : I shall soon polish him off! (*Exit*).

After a few moments a rushing sound is heard and the chair in which MARK *is seated tips over backwards and, with a scream, he disappears. After a short pause the chair returns to its normal position—empty.* (*Note : a stage trap is not required for this effect. See production notes on page* 87).

TODD *returns, examining the string of pearls which he holds in his hand. The chair starts to jerk up and down and* TODD *retreats downstage right, frightened.*

Todd : What is this ? Can I believe my eyes—some ghostly trick ? (*Passes a hand across his brow*). The chair has life of its own. Terror bedews my forehead. No, no—courage Sweeney. It is only that the mechanism in some manner is disorganised. And remember, Sweeney—the string of pearls, the string of pearls (*crossing to down left*). When a boy, the thirst of avarice was first awakened by the fair gift of a farthing—that farthing soon became a pound—that pound a hundred pounds—so to a thousand pounds until I said to myself, I will possess a hundred thousand pounds. The string of pearls will complete the sum. (*Starts*) Who's there ?

He moves to above the down right door, where he hides. TOBIAS *comes into the room slowly and is pounced on by* TODD *from behind.*

Todd : Tobias, Tobias, how long were you peeping through the door before you came in ? How long boy—how long ? Speak—and speak the truth or your last hour has come!

Tobias : Peeping, sir ?

Todd : Yes, peeping—don't repeat my words, but answer at once. You'll find it better for you in the end.

Tobias : Please sir, I wasn't peeping at all sir, please sir.

Todd (*looking carefully at* TOBIAS *and changing his manner*) : Well, well, if you did peep, what then ? I only wanted to know, that's all. It was quite a joke wasn't it—quite funny (*laughs loudly*). Though rather odd, eh ? Why don't you laugh, you dog ? Come now, there's no harm done, tell me what you thought about, at once. We'll be merry over it, —very merry—eh ?

Tobias : Yes, sir, very merry, but I really don't know what you mean.

Todd: I mean nothing at all, eh? What! (*knock off right*) Who's that at the door?

Tobias (*looking off right*): It's only the black servant of the gentleman who came here to be shaved this morning.

Todd: Tell the fellow his master's not here. Go . . . let him seek elsewhere . . . he's not here . . . do you hear me? Do you hear me? (*Aside*) I know I shall have to polish that boy off. (*He whets his razor on his hand—as he does so* TOBIAS *discovers* MARK's *hat which he hides behind his back*).

Tobias (*aside*): This is most odd. 'Tis improbable that he would go without giving notice to his servant. (*Aloud*) But suppose the man won't go?

Todd (*aloud*): Well then I shall have to polish him off, too.

Exit TOBIAS. TODD *looks through doorway right.*

Todd: Who's this approaching now? Ah, if my memory does not deceive me, it could be Jean Parmine, the famous lapidary, the very man I need. Fortune is evidently favouring me.

Enter JEAN PARMINE *from down right.*

Parmine: Good evening neighbour; I would have you shave me.

Todd: Your servant, Mr Parmine, would you be seated in this chair (*indicates centre chair*) and I'll attend to you at once.

Parmine (*sitting*): Thank you neighbour.

Todd (*as he puts towel round* PARMINE's *neck*): Tell me my friend, do you not deal in precious stones?

Parmine: Yes, I do, but is it not rather late for a bargain? Do you wish to buy or sell?

Todd: To sell.

Parmine: Hum! I dare say it's something not in my line. The only orders I get are for pearls and they are not in the market at the present time.

Todd: But it is pearls, I have for sale—and nothing but pearls. I mean to keep all my diamonds, garnets and rubies.

Parmine: The deuce you do! What, do you mean to say you have any of them? Be off with you, I'm too old to joke and I'm waiting for my supper.

Todd: Will you look at the pearls I have?

Parmine: Where are they?
Todd: I have them here (*produces a casket and gives it to* PARMINE).
Parmine (*examining the pearls*): Real—by heaven—all real—every single one of them!
Todd: You don't need to tell me, I know they are real. Now then, will you deal with me or not?
Parmine: Now that I look at them again I begin to doubt their worth. Let me examine them a little more closely. Ah, yes, as I feared, counterfeit. But they are cunningly done. Indeed they are so well done that for the curiosity of the thing I will give you—fifty pounds.
Todd: Fifty pounds? Now who is the one who is joking I wonder? Ah well, that's it then; we cannot deal today.
Parmine: Stay! I will give you a hundred. Now that is more than they are worth but they have taken my fancy and I will offer you more than their value.
Todd: Hark ye, friend, it neither suits my inclination nor my time to stand here haggling with you. I know the value of pearls, and as a matter of ordinary business I will sell them to you so that you can get a handsome profit for yourself.
Parmine: Well then, since you know far more than I gave you credit for, and this is to be a downright business transaction, I think I can find a customer who will pay eleven thousand pounds for them. If so, I have no objection to advance the sum of eight thousand pounds.
Todd: I am content. Let me have the money by tomorrow morning at the very latest.
Parmine: Not so hasty my friend, not so hasty. There are certain matters of considerable importance that we have to discuss before we come to any definite agreement.
Todd: What matters pray? I have offered you the pearls. You have been at great pains to assess their true value and there would appear no further obstacle to completing the deal.
Parmine: You must know that a string of pearls is not to be purchased like a few ounces of old silver and that the vendor must give every satisfaction as to how he came by them.
Todd (*aside*): I see I shall have to polish him off, (*aloud*)

Psha! man, who will question you, who are known to be in the trade?

Parmine: That's as may be, but I don't see why I should give you the full value of an article without evidence to prove your title to it.

Todd: What you are saying, my friend, in other words is that you don't care how I came to possess the property provided I sell it to you at a thief's price, but if, on the contrary I want their real value, you mean to be particular.

Parmine (*forcefully*): I'll tell you what I mean and in no uncertain terms. I strongly suspect that you have no right to dispose of the pearls and to satisfy myself I shall insist upon your accompanying me to a magistrate.

Todd: And what road shall you take?

Parmine: The right road, Mr Todd, the right road!

Todd (*who has moved to the upstage right door*): Then off you go, Mr Parmine, off you go! (*springing into the next room*) Goodbye, goodbye, goodbye!

The chair turns over and from the next room TODD *is heard roaring with laughter. The chair returns but instead of being empty it is occupied by* SMITH *who is sitting in it smiling when* TODD *returns.*

Smith: Not goodbye, Mr Todd, not at all. Not goodbye but how do you do, dear Mr Todd.

Todd (*standing aghast for a moment, then speaking slowly and menacingly*): So, you know the secret of the gravestone, too? (SMITH *nods and smiles*) It is enough. Your bill is paid.

Smith: But you have forgotten one thing. It still requires a receipt, Mr Todd.

Todd: I suppose it was you too who was responsible for the sudden liveliness of my chair just now, eh? (SMITH *smiles and nods again*) I fancy you are just a little too clever, Mr Smith. I do not like to have such a clever mechanic in my confidence. It does not altogether suit.

TODD *draws a pistol from his pocket and fires at* SMITH *who falls back into the chair with blood pouring from his forehead.*

Todd : Ha, Mr Clever Smith, you won't do much thinking now, I fancy, with that bleeding head. You can take all your cleverness down below now; you can have another little ride in this very particular chair of yours. It ought to work well now that its master is sitting in it. (*He moves towards upstage right door, screaming with laughter*).

CURTAIN

ACT ONE

SCENE III

THE BREAKFAST PARLOUR IN THE HOUSE OF JASPER OAKLEY.

There is a small table right centre stage with a chair behind it and another to right of it. A decorated draught screen stands down left. (Note: to facilitate set changes this scene can be played in front of a traverse curtain or drop cloth).

When the curtain rises, JOHANNA *is discovered seated right of the table looking sadly at a miniature portrait.*

Johanna: Oh Mark, Mark! Why do you thus desert me when I have relied so abundantly on your true affection? Oh, why have you not sent me some token of your existence and of your continual love? The merest, the slightest word would have been sufficient, and I would have been happy. (*She rises and sings*):

WHERE HAVE YOU GONE?

(JOHANNA)

REFRAIN I

Where have you gone, where are you now?
Why have you deserted me?
Did you forget our solemn vow,
Whilst sailing across the sea?
Never a word a line from you,
To show that our love was true.
Where have you gone, where are you now?
Why have you parted from me?

VERSE

My lonely soul is aching,
My hours are spent in tears.
My heart is nigh to breaking,
I've missed you all these years.

REFRAIN II

Where have you gone, where are you now?
Why have you deserted me?
I cannot live without you near,

Sail back across the sea.
Without a doubt you surely know
That darling I love you so.
My heart will yearn for your return
'Til you come back safe to me.

During the last two lines of the song she sinks into the chair right and as the song ends she bursts into tears. The sound of footsteps on gravel is heard off right.

Johanna: Hark, what was that? (*rising and looking off right*) I'm sure I heard footseps beneath the chamber window. As I live, a man in the garden. He holds a white rose in his hand; that should be an emblem of faith and purity. At every hazard I will address the stranger. He may bring tidings of him I so well love. (*She opens the door and* COLONEL JEFFREY *enters*).

Jeffrey: I have the honour of speaking to Miss Johanna Oakley?

Johanna: Yes, sir, and you are the messenger of Mark Ingestre?

Jeffrey: I am.

Johanna: Oh, sir, your looks are so sad and serious, it would appear that you are about to announce some dreadful misfortune that has occurred. Tell me if it is not so? Speak to me sir, speak at once, I beseech you, or my heart will break.

Jeffrey: Let me pray you, lady, to subdue this passion of grief, and listen with all patience to what I shall unfold. There is much to hear and much to speculate upon, and if from all that I have learnt, I cannot—indeed I dare not, tell you Mark Ingestre lives, I shrink in a like fashion from telling you he is no more.

Johanna: Speak again, sir, speak again! Say those words for a second time. There is hope then, there is hope?

Jeffrey: There is hope, and it is better that your mind should receive the first shock of the probability of your lover's death than that from the first you should expect too much and then have those expectations cruelly destroyed.

Johanna: This is kind of you, and if I cannot thank you as

I ought, I am certain you will attribute that to its rightful cause—the fact that I am in a state of too great affliction to do so.

Jeffrey : That I would, my dear lady, if the expression of your gratitude were required, but I would assure you that it is not.

Johanna : Tell me the news, my dear sir, I implore you.

Jeffrey : You are aware that a quarrel with his uncle caused him to embark on an adventure in the Indian Seas ?

Johanna : Too well. Alas, it was on my account he sacrificed himself.

Jeffrey : Nay, dear lady, he did not sacrifice himself. Good fortune attended that enterprise, and Mark Ingestre amongst others returned to his native land a wealthy and extremely prosperous merchant. He showed me on our homeward voyage a string of pearls of immense value, which he told me that he intended for you.

Johanna : For me ?

Jeffrey : Yes, he was to have presented them to you yesterday. In fact when we reached the River Thames, only three days since, he left the vessel for that very purpose.

Johanna : Alas, he never came!

Jeffrey : No, from all inquiries we can make, and from information we have been able to obtain, it seems that he disappeared somewhere in Fleet Street.

Johanna : Disappeared ?

Jeffrey : Yes, we have been able to trace him to Temple Stairs and from thence to a barber's shop kept by a man named Sweeney Todd, but beyond, we have no clue whatsoever.

Johanna : Does not this barber, this Sweeney Todd know anything ? Has he been asked if Mr Ingestre happened to say for whence he was bound when he left his establishment ?

Jeffrey : He has indeed been asked that very question but professes to know nothing of Mark Ingestre's commitments beyond that in his barber's shop. It would appear that . . .

Johanna : Hush—someone is coming. 'Tis my mother's voice. You had better not be seen at present. Conceal yourself till I can speak further with you. (*She indicates the screen, behind which* JEFFREY *hides*).

Enter JASPER OAKLEY, *a meek, timid man, followed by* MRS OAKLEY, *a large domineering woman.*

Mrs Oakley (*moving over to* JOHANNA *who is standing right of screen*): How is this child? You look pale. If you are ill, I must speak positively about you to Dr Lupin.

Jasper: Dr Lupin may be all very well in his way as a p-p-parson, but I really don't see what he can have to do with Johanna looking p-p-pale.

Mrs Oakley: Let me tell you, Mr Oakley, that a pious man has to do with everything and everybody.

Jasper: Then he must indeed be the most intolerable b-b-bore that has ever lived on this earth and I don't wonder at the stories I have heard about him.

Mrs Oakley: And pray, Mr Oakley, what stories have you heard about the good Dr Lupin?

Jasper (*retreating to downstage right below screen*): I have heard on the very b-b-best authority that he has been forcibly removed from some people's houses and some go as far as to state that he had been kicked out.

Mrs Oakley (*crossing* JOHANNA *and bearing down on* JASPER): If the sainted Dr Lupin has been kicked, Mr Oakley, I can assure you that he glories in it. Dr Lupin likes to suffer for the faith and if he were made a martyr I can think of nothing that would give him greater pleasure.

Jasper: It would not give him half the p-p-pleasure it would give me.

Mrs Oakley: I understand your insinuation, Mr Oakley, oh yes, I understand it well enough. You would like nothing better than to see him murdered on account of his holiness. But, let me tell you though you say these words so bravely now you won't say as much to the lamb of peace when he comes to our house for tea this afternoon.

Jasper: To tea, Mrs Oakley? Have I not told you over and over again that I will not have this man in my house?

Mrs Oakley (*forcing* JASPER *into corner*): And haven't I told you, Mr Oakley, twice that number of times, that he shall come to tea? I have told you, Mr Oakley, until indeed I am tired of telling you. Anyway I have asked him now, and it cannot be altered.

Jasper: But my dear, you fail to understand, I have decreed that he shall not cross my threshold and that as far as I am concerned makes an end of it.

Mrs Oakley (*aggressively*): But not as far as I am concerned, Mr Oakley.

Jasper: But my dear . . . (*he sings*):

I'M THE MASTER

(JASPER)

I'm the master of this house,
I'm the ruler of my spouse.
What I say is always done,
Both by daughter and by son.

I'm the master of them all,
They're all at my beck and call,
Family, servants all bow low,
I serve neither friend nor foe.

Undisputed king am I,
They don't argue, never try;
For they know I won't be crossed.
I am boss and won't be bossed.

When I speak all others stop,
They're aware of who's on top,
They respect the right I've got,
Anyway they all talk rot.

So you see just how I stand,
I'm supreme throughout my land,
Others tremble and obey.
HE'LL NOT COME TO TEA I SAY!

Mrs Oakley: We will not discuss the matter further, Mr Oakley, I have decided. Johanna, (*sinking into chair right*) I think my old complaint, the beating of the heart, is coming on. I know what produces it—your father's brutality. I must retire and compose my nerves with a little cherry brandy.

JOHANNA *assists her out right.*

Jasper (*aside*): B-b-bless my soul, I have been too p-precipitate, I fear that one day my violent temper will cause the death of the poor woman. I must offer her crumbs of comfort, as Dr Lupin would say. Damn Dr Lupin! (*Goes out right*).

JOHANNA *returns and* JEFFREY *comes out from behind screen.*

Jeffrey: I fear that it is necessary, Miss Oakley, that I now leave you but I want you to make me a promise.

Johanna: You have but to name it, my dear sir.

Jeffrey: You must promise to meet me . . .

Johanna: When and where?

Jeffrey: At the hour of six this day week, in the Temple Gardens. I ask this of you, my dear Miss Oakley, because I am resolved to exercise every power I possess to discover what has become of Mark Ingestre, in whose fate I am sure I have succeeded in interesting you, although you care so little for the string of pearls he intended to present to you.

Johanna: The pearls! I do, indeed, care little for them—so little that in truth it may be said to amount to nothing.

Jeffrey: Yet it is well not to despise a gift so precious. If you can yourself do nothing with them, there are surely some others you know upon whom they would bestow great happiness.

Johanna: A string of pearls—how can a string of pearls bring great happiness?

Jeffrey: Your mind is so occupied by your grief, Miss Oakley, that you quite forget that such strings are of great value. I have seen these pearls that we speak of, and can assure you they are, in themselves, a fortune.

Johanna: I suppose it is too much for human nature to expect two blessings at once. I had the fond warm heart that loved me, without the fortune that would have enabled us to live in comfort and now, when that is perchance, almost within my grasp, the heart which was by far the most costly possession lies buried in an untimely grave—its bright influence, its glorious and noble aspirations quenched for ever.

Jeffrey: All is not yet lost, Miss Oakley—we must hope and pray that we will succeed in finding your lost love again this side of the grave.

Johanna : With all my heart I pray it may be so, with all my heart.

Jeffrey : You will meet me then as I request, to hear if I have any news for you?

Johanna : I have the will to do so, but Heaven knows only if I may have the power.

Jeffrey : What do you mean?

Music.

Johanna : I cannot tell what a week's anxiety may do. I do not know but a sick bed may be my resting place until I exchange it for a coffin. I feel now my strength fail me and I am scarcely able to totter to my chamber. Even now I am weak with apprehension and near mortal woe. Farewell, dear sir, farewell, kind gentleman, I owe you my best thanks as well for the trouble you have taken as for the kindly manner in which you have detailed to me what has passed.

Music ends.

Jeffrey : There are no thanks due to me I assure you, my dear young lady. And now I must bid you adieu, with the hope of meeting you again in one week's time. (*A voice is heard off right,* JOHANNA *moves to* JEFFREY).

Johanna : Someone else is coming.

JEFFREY *exchanges a glance with* JOHANNA *and retires behind the screen again as the door opens and* DR LUPIN *enters.*

Johanna : Lupin here! (*aside*) How unfortunate!

Lupin : Yes, maiden. I am that chosen vessel whom the profane call 'Old Mealy Mouth'. I come hither at the bidding of thy respected mother to partake of a vain mixture which rejoiceth in the name of 'tea'.

JOHANNA *attempts to move right but is stopped by* LUPIN.

Johanna : You will allow me a free passage from the room if you please, Dr Lupin.

Lupin : Thou art very disrespectful, but I will not snub thee, virgin, because thou knowest not the honour that is intended for thee.

Johanna (*aside*) : What can he mean? (*To* LUPIN) I do not understand you, Dr Lupin.

Lupin : Then I will acquaint thee with the full meaning of

"Verily you speak truth, 'tis fat indeed!"

DR LUPIN *and* MRS POORLEAN

"We are reunited, never to be parted again!"

JOHANNA *and* MARK

Fleet Street

Sweeney Todd's Shop

The Bakehouse

The Madhous

A Court of Justice

Entrance to Newgate Prison

my words. Thy mother hath decided that I take thee unto my bosom, even as a wedded wife.

Johanna: Absurd! Have you been drinking?

Lupin: I never drink, save when the spirit waxeth faint. (*He takes a bottle from his pocket and drinks*). 'Tis an ungodly practice (*drinks again*). Thou wilt shortly become as bone of my bone, flesh of my flesh. Thou dost not deserve such an honour (*drinks*).

Johanna: We do not get all we deserve in this world, Dr Lupin.

Lupin: True, indeed true (*offers bottle*). Let me offer you spiritual consolation, hic!

Johanna: Bless me, you have hiccups.

Lupin: Yes, I rather think I have, a little. Is it not a shame that one so pious should have the hiccups? Hic! Hic! Damn the hiccups, that is, I mean damn all backsliders!

Johanna (*aside*): The miserable hypocrite.

Lupin: I can bear it no longer, not even another instant. The fire of love rageth; it consumeth my very vitals. Peradventure I may extinguish the flame by the moisture of those ruby lips. Nay, I am resolved (*he siezes* JOHANNA).

Johanna: Unhand me, you ruffian—unhand me, or repent it!

JEFFREY *comes from behind the screen and commences to hit* LUPIN *with the scabbard of his sword.* LUPIN *rushes across to the downstage right door.*

Lupin: Help! Murder! Verily I am assailed! Robbers! Fire! Help!

As LUPIN *reaches the door, pursued by* JEFFREY, *he is met by all the members of the household brandishing brooms, mops, frying pans, etc. He turns and is chased off left with the household in hot pursuit—Music.*

CURTAIN

ACT TWO

SCENE ONE

THE PARLOUR BEHIND MRS LOVETT'S PIE SHOP IN BELL YARD. *There is a table left centre with a chair to left and to right of it. Downstage right an old fashioned stove with a kettle and a teapot on it. When the curtain rises* MRS LOVETT *is seated right of the table knitting.*

Boy : (*shouting from off right*) : Mrs Lovett! Mrs Lovett!
Mrs Lovett : What is it you want boy ?
Boy : I want two twopenny pies for Mrs Widdle-Waddle.
Mrs Lovett : You're too late—all sold—not one left. Go away! (*Aside*) Heigho, I feel lonely. How I wish that at this very moment one of my admirers would call upon me, just to while away the tedious moments. (*Rising, and moving down left*) Let me see now, which one might it be ? I wonder what the prospects of Major Bounce are ? He's tolerably good-looking although middle-aged. Then there's Mr Mason Travers, who is forever forcing his attentions upon me. I know not whether I could bear to be with him for any length of time. Indeed I think I would prefer my own solitude unless it were very dark, for he is a revolting looking man, no more than five feet tall with one eye that looks east and the other I swear due west. Then there's Mr Lupin, a very nice man it is true, but he will persist in talking of such melancholy subjects.
(*Moving right to look out of window*) What a short sharp shower to be sure! Fortunate for me that I did not pay my intended visit to Mr Sweeney Todd. I should have caught my death of cold.
(*Knock at door*).
Ah, a knock at the door! Some of those troublesome customers again. Go away, I've no pies left, be off with you I say!
(*Knock*).
Another knock! Ah well, I suppose I had better find out who it is. (*Looking out of window again*).
Why, if it isn't Mr Lupin. I must make haste and let him in,

or the poor gentleman will be wet through. (*She goes out right*).

Mrs Lovett (*returning with* DR LUPIN *who is shaking his umbrella*) : A thousand pardons, Mr Lupin, for keeping you outside so long. But the fact is I took you for a customer. Give me your umbrella, sit down and take something warm or in truth you will die of cold.

Lupin : Yes, dear sister, I bear this misfortune, like all others, with fortitude; believing that our suffering here will all, in a future world be changed to peace and happiness. Yea verily and I say unto thee, the acts of the wicked will call forth the wrath they deserve. (*Sits left of table*).

Mrs Lovett : Certainly, therefore I beg you will take a drop of tea with a little something in it to just keep out the cold.

She pours out two cups of tea and adds a minute amount of rum to each cup from a bottle which she leaves on the table. She returns the teapot to the hob and while her back is turned, LUPIN *tips away the tea and fills his cup with rum and is nearly caught doing it, but greets* MRS LOVETT *with a bland smile.*

Lupin : Dear sister, you are indeed an angel. Ah me, tea, what a blessing it is Mrs L. What should we do without it, dear sister?

Mrs Lovett : Ah indeed, Mr Lupin. (*Sits right of table*).

Lupin : Call me brother, dear sister, call me brother, for we are all brothers and sisters in this wicked world, are we not?

Mrs Lovett : Oh, Mr Lupin . . . won't you draw your chair a little closer?

Lupin : I will indeed, dear sister, I will indeed. (*Moves chair to behind table, nearer to* MRS LOVETT). Tell me, Mrs L., is it true that thou hast gathered unto thyself much of the mammon of unrighteousness by the sale of these same pieces of manna which the ungodly call dough, wrapped around the flesh of the fatted calf?

Mrs Lovett (*coyly*) : Oh mister brother, what a lovely way of saying pies!

Lupin : Call me brother, my sister. Verily, 'Mr Brother', is an abomination. Now, let us talk again of these pies of yours. If reports are true . . .

Mrs Lovett : Oh, brother, let us not talk of pies. Remember that all day and all night I think of nothing but pies and sometimes even when I am in bed at night and should be sleeping the untroubled sleep of the innocent, I am haunted in my dreams by pies. Remember that all day I smell pies and kneed dough for pies and take twopences for pies.

Lupin : Verily, sister, it is a delicious text. Lo, the smell of gravy haunteth my nostrils and my soul quivers with delight.

Mrs Lovett (*moving very close*) : Then would you like a pie—brother ?

Lupin : My soul fainteth, yea my stomach crieth out. Oh, my sister, oh, my beloved, verily I would partake of thy pies!

MRS LOVETT *goes off right to fetch the pie. While she is away he helps himself to some more rum from the bottle and sings :*

VERILY, VERILY SO

(DR LUPIN)

Though it's not nice, I have a vice.
Verily, verily so.
Thou wilt agree when thou dost see.
Verily, verily so.
I have the urge—my soul to purge.
Verily, verily so.
Alas and alack 'tis very black.
Verily, verily so.
If thou canst guess, I must confess.
Verily, verily so.
So I'll begin to bare my sin.
Verily, verily so.
Ere Heaven's fall I must tell all.
Verily, verily so.
Perdition come! I love the rum.
Verily, verily so.
Not just a drop, I cannot stop.
Verily, verily no.
I like a lot, I'm just a sot.
Verily, verily woe.
Gallons of rum lie in my 'tum'.
Verily, verily so.

Soon it must tire, I will expire.
Verily, verily oh!
Why did I fall ?—no hope at all.
Verily, verily cry.
Ah wicked me, pickled I'll be.
But oh, what a nice way to die!

On the last line of the song he attempts to drink from the bottle but finds it empty and sinks into the chair right of table clutching the empty bottle.

MRS LOVETT *returns with a pie on a plate which she sets before* DR LUPIN *who rolls up his sleeves and ties a handkerchief round his neck.*

Lupin (*with knife and fork raised*) : Nay, sister, of a surety this is not a twopenny pie ?

Mrs Lovett : Oh no, Mr Lupin, oh no, this is a very special pie indeed such as I keep for callers and very dear friends.

Lupin : And tell me, sister, is there a good profit to be made on a twopenny pie ? Dost thou put in a pennyworth of the fat of calf ?

Mrs Lovett : Now, Mr Lupin, how do you imagine I live ? I most certainly do not put in so much as a pennyworth.

Lupin : How much dost thou put in then ?

Mrs Lovett : I put in a farthingsworth and not an iota more.

Lupin : I perceive that thou art a shrewd business woman, dear sister. (*smacking his lips*) Verily a magnificent pie. Of truth thou art a woman in a thousand. And tell me more of the making of thy pies. How much flour puttest thou in a twopenny pie ?

Mrs Lovett : A halfpennyworth, Mr Lupin.

Lupin : And whence cometh thy flour, my beloved ?

Mrs Lovett : I buy it from Miller Brown.

Lupin : And Miller Brown has nearby his mill certain cavities in the earth containing a certain white substance known as chalk, hath he not, sister ?

Mrs Lovett : Miller Brown is a highly respectable merchant, Mr Lupin.

Lupin : Hoity-toity, did I say aught else ? (*Finishing the pie*).

Ah, sister, what a pie, what a pie was that. Behold my heart yearneth after thy beauty; behold a great love welleth up in my soul. (*Rising and moving to left of* MRS LOVETT). Wilt thou take my hand? Tell me, dear sister, hast thou what the wicked call a stocking?

Mrs Lovett: And supposing that I have—what of that to you?

Lupin: Hark, I will whisper (*puts his mouth to her ear and in a hoarse whisper*): Is it near thy bed?

Mrs Lovett: Oh, brother, brother you mustn't. (LUPIN *whispers again, this time inaudibly*) Oh, Mr Lupin, you are a naughty man!

Lupin: Hist, my beloved, wilt thou call me Lupy now? (*holds her hand*).

Mrs Lovett: Oh, Mr Lupin!

Lupin: Lupy, I say, Lupy! (*draws her closer to him*). And wilt meet me at twelve o'clock near Temple Bar? For the work of the Lord calleth his servant and I must be gone. (*In a hoarse whisper as he goes*) Twelve o'clock then, lovey, near Temple Bar (*goes off right.*)

Mrs Lovett: Oh . . . Oh . . . Lupy! (*sinks into chair right*) Lupy!!!!

CURTAIN

ACT TWO

SCENE TWO

SWEENEY TODD'S SHOP

LUPIN *enters right and proceeds to look around the room with caution.*

Lupin : Verily I believe this Sweeney to be a man of sin. I have a mind to test his wickedness. Yea, I believe that he hath secrets that he will buy at a great price, for it is rumoured much abroad that his wealth is very great and of a surety it is well that the children of the Lord should partake of the ill-gotten gains of the wicked and strip the robber of his spoil.

Enter TODD *from door down right.*

Ah, good evening to you, Mr Todd. I would have you shave me.

Todd : Certainly; pray sit down (*aside*) I wonder if this one's worth polishing off. (LUPIN *sits in chair left*). No, not that one please, this one over here. (LUPIN *sits in chair right*). No, not that one, this one here. I shall be able to attend to you ever so much quicker in this chair. The light is much better and I shall have you polished off in no time at all. (LUPIN *crosses to centre chair, treading cautiously. When he is seated* TODD *puts the towel round his neck and begins to lather him furiously*).

Lupin : Please - p - p - please, Mr Todd, not so hard, not so hard.

Todd : What ? (*lathers him even harder*).

Lupin : Pray, Mr Todd, remember that we had a most bountiful collection at the meeting yester-eve and that the man of God can well afford that gracious offering which is known to the unrighteous as a 'tip'.

Todd (*aside*) : Damn me! It seems he is worth polishing off!

Lupin : Pray shave me carefully, Mr Todd, for I am to meet a wealthy heiress I would fain make the wife of my bosom.

Todd : A wealthy heiress eh ? And may I be so bold as to enquire the name of this most worthy lady ?

Lupin : Of a surety, she is not unknown to you.

Todd : Indeed, and what is her name, pray ?

Lupin : Verily, sir, that is neither here nor there.
Todd (*aside*) : Faith I know where he'll be if he doesn't answer my question. (*To* LUPIN) 'Tis of no consequence. It is of no real interest to me whom she may be. (*holds razor aloft as if to cut* LUPIN'S *throat*).
Lupin (*shrinking back in the chair*) : 'Tis this Mrs Lovett who owns a pie shop that the Lord has blessed with a trade bountiful and ever-flowing.
Todd (*in consternation*) : What d'ye say? Then you ARE going to be polished off. (*He hurries into the next room.* LUPIN, *his face covered with lather, towel round his neck, jumps out of the chair, runs down left and watches the chair turn over*).
Lupin (*forgetting himself in his excitement*) : So that's how you do it! You'll pay blood-money for this, Mr Todd.

TODD *comes back and rushes at* LUPIN *in a rage with razor raised.* LUPIN *evades him and there is a chase round the chairs to the accompaniment of music while the following dialogue is spoken.*

Todd : By God, I'll polish you off you devil!
Lupin : Keep away from me you fiend. I'll have you hung, drawn and quartered!
Todd : I'll tear you to ribbons! I'll cut your tongue out!
Lupin : Curse you, you inhuman wretch!
Todd : When I get hold of you I'll shave you so close your own mother wouldn't know you from a billiard ball.
Lupin (*as he reaches the door right*) : Help! Murder! Arson! Thieves! (*He rushes screaming off the stage pursued by* TODD *with razor*).

A silence descends. The lights fade to blackout and a green spot covers the area of the centre chair, which tips back to its normal position. Seated in the chair is MARK INGESTRE, *his clothes torn and dishevelled and with blood dripping from wounds on his head. Slowly and with great difficulty he drags himself from the chair. As he staggers downstage the green light fades and the stage lighting comes up to half.*

Mark : Have my senses left me, do I dream of horrors unparalleled, or is my existence a reality? I remember this place. The man who invited me here stood yonder and this is the chair on which I sat (*examines it*) . . . afterwards, falling into

the depths below. Merciful heaven! This piece of machinery to which a chain is fixed either side is a contrivance for the purpose of murder and robbery. My pocket book gone, my string of pearls—all lost! The facts are clear enough. The owner of this shop is a robber and an assassin, but I have not quite fallen a victim to his inhuman designs, for though weak and defenceless I will sell my life dearly.
(*He goes to the door right and tries it*). It will not yield. Never mind, I'll soon force it open when I find an intrument fit for the purpose (*moves upstage right*). What is here? Another door? This leads to the room into which the scoundrel entered before I was thrown into the cellar below. (*He goes to the chair and examines it more closely*).
The mystery is explained. A bolt is here communicating with the spring from yonder room, and at the murderer's will his unsuspecting victims are launched into eternity. Someone is at the door. Perhaps it is the assassin himself. Murderer, I am prepared for you.

He hides behind the down right door. After a moment the door begins to open very slowly and in the half-light a figure is seen upon which MARK *springs.*

Tobias: Help! Leave me be! Help!
Mark: Silence, another word and 'tis the last you will utter.
Tobias: Merciful Heaven! The sailor, the owner of the string of pearls.
Mark: The same. And let me tell you a man who is determined to leave this murderer's den, but not until he has dragged the owner to prison. Where is he? Tell me this instant or I swear you will regret it for the rest of your days.
Tobias: I know not where he is. I expected to find him here.
Mark: You lie. You know full well where he is, for I believe you to be in league with the villain.
Tobias: Indeed I am not. Say rather that I am in his power.
Mark: You swear that?
Tobias: With all my heart. He has me in his foul clutches and I desire most earnestly to escape.
Mark: Then assist me to bring him to the hands of justice.

Tobias : I will! I will! Only tell me how to act that we may bring that about.

Mark : Then listen to me and mark well what I have to tell you.

Tobias : Yes, only tell me, for I have great fear of him.

Mark : Fetch the police officers here. I will stay here and await the murderer's coming and secure him until assistance arrives.

Tobias : I will run all the way, never fear. The police officers will be here within these five minutes.

Exit TOBIAS *running down right.*

Mark (*alone*) : Now to wait until the villain appears. I think I hear footsteps. He is coming. No . . . they have gone past. My head is swimming, my heart beats fast, but it is not fear. Spring together all my senses, there is still work to be done. Steel yourself sinews, there is fighting to come (*his voice trembles*). Only, it's growing darker, I cannot see. There is blood dripping in front of my eyes. Where has all the light gone? I must sit down, I must rest. I must sleep a long, long, sleep . . . (*staggers about the stage*). Which chair is this? Why is it so dark? . . . it may be the fatal chair. Why have my eyes gone? Hush! I think I can hear his approach. I can't see, I can't see . . . for blood . . . (*He stumbles into the chair which slowly tips back as the lights fade to blackout*).

Enter TODD *with a lamp which he holds so that his face is illuminated from below. He comes downstage centre and sings :*

I'M EVIL

(SWEENEY TODD)

When I was a little lad,
I was often very bad.
When a youth I turned to crime,
And now I'm evil all the time.
I'm evil, I'm evil, as evil can be,
I doubt if there's anyone as evil as me.

I regret the years I spent,
Working hard to pay the rent.
Now I've got a better plan,
I've become an evil man.
I'm evil, I'm evil as evil can be,
I doubt if there's anyone as evil as me.

I remember as a boy,
Kindness often gave me joy.
Now, I'm very proud to say,
I do my evil deed each day.
I'm evil, I'm evil, as evil can be,
I doubt if there's anyone as evil as me.

What a wicked man I've been,
Quite the worst you've ever seen.
All my friends I've lost I fear,
I cut their throats from ear to ear.
I'm evil, I'm evil, as evil can be,
I doubt if there's anyone as evil as me.

When my life of crime is o'er
And on earth I'm bad no more,
When my bones they've laid away,
On my stone I hope they'll say:
He was evil, so evil, as evil can be,
We doubt if there was anyone as evil as 'he'.

(*Encore*)

I'm afraid I can't resist
Adding victims to my list,
So if you should fail to boo
Then the next one could be you.
I'm evil, I'm evil as evil can be,
I'm certain there's no one as evil as me.

Todd (*moving upstage to put lamp on cupboard as stage lighting is brought up*): That ranting parson has escaped me, but I fear no man of his kidney. A little money, an offering he will call it . . . blackmail I should say . . . merely a temporary disbursement to be returned along with all the other effects of the legator. Ha! ha! a pretty jest. The legator! And when he has been polished off . . . poor Lupin . . .

Enter MRS LOVETT *right.*

Ah, Mistress Lovett, rather late for a call is it not? Still as a mere matter of friendship I'll overlook the indiscretion on this occasion (*moving downstage centre*). And can I do anything for you?

Mrs Lovett (*moving to his right*): My mind is disturbed, Todd, I am most unhappy.

Todd: What is it that troubles you, Mistress Lovett?

Mrs Lovett: The wicked manner of our lives darkens every hour and colours all my dreams, Todd, colours them with blood! Can there not be a change? Can we not reform our ways and live good righteous lives?

Todd (*going to her and seizing her wrist in an iron grip*): What do you mean?

Mrs Lovett: Don't, Todd, you hurt me.

Todd: Then tell me, tell me exactly what you are talking about.

Mrs Lovett (*trembling*): I am talking of William Grant, he died last night.

Todd: And who may William Grant be?

Mrs Lovett: But you know him, he was my baker, Todd.

Todd: But my dear Mistress Lovett, your baker's name was Jones.

Mrs Lovett (*bursting into tears*): He had a nice face that Jones had, Todd, a lovely face. But he got discontented. Surely you remember?

Todd: There are so many of them one gets confused, Mistress Lovett. I vow I have the greatest difficulty in keeping track of them all. But never mind, dry those tears, little cry baby. There is nothing to upset yourself about. (*Pushing her down right*).

Mrs Lovett (*firmly*): Todd, I have come here, not to be called a cry baby, but to tell you there has to be an end. I have come to tell you that the pie shop in Bell Yard is going to be closed. My conscience is aroused, I begin to have bad dreams.

I tell you, Sweeney Todd, demon in human shape that you are, that you and I are shortly to see the last of each other.

Todd: My heart goes out to you in sympathy, my dear Mistress Lovett, but you must be tired of standing all this long while. Let me implore you my dear Mistress Lovett to take a seat. (*Pushing her upstage to centre chair*).

Mrs Lovett (*backing away from chair*): In THAT chair. Do you think I am such a fool, Sweeney Todd? (TODD *takes her wrist and begins deliberately to twist it—she writhes in agony*) Please, please, Todd, my dear . . .

Todd: You see, Mistress Lovett, I know how to control you—as I know how to control all women. Believe me, my dear, the management of women is much like the management of horses—force judiciously applied. (*He drags her around the stage collecting the chairs right and left as he does so and places them side-by-side downstage centre*).

Come let us sit down my dear and talk like old friends (*pushing her into a chair and sitting on her right, still holding her wrist*). You know you did not mean what you said just now. Come, come, think a little, be reasonable, Mistress Lovett.

Mrs Lovett: Pray leave go my hand. You are crushing it. Almost I can hear the bones crackle.

Todd (*complacently*): I have been always noted for my strength.

Mrs Lovett: I want to go out, I must breathe the clean air. Let me go! Let me go!

Todd: Air, did you say—come I will open a window. (*Rises and takes her right to open a window*).

Mrs Lovett: Let me go, let me go. I must go outside.

Todd: Come, come, my dear Mistress Lovett, why this hurry to be out at this time of the evening?

Mrs Lovett: Let me go I say, unhand me you wretch!

Todd: Nay, nay, we shall sit here quietly and talk of your troubles. (*Pulls her back to centre stage and sits her in chair again*). You were most anxious to do so but a short while since. Let me see now, what was the subject of our discourse. Ah, yes, you were speaking of the unexpected demise of this—let me see what was his name? Not Jones—no that was not it. What was it now? (*The church clock begins to strike twelve*). Ah, cry, cry on. That is right, it will do you good. There is nothing calculated to do so much good to a poor frail woman as a really nice cry.

Mrs Lovett: Let me go, let me go!

Todd: Ah, ha, midnight! Now is the right time for a heart to heart talk.

They sing:

DEAR MISTRESS L.

(SWEENEY TODD AND MRS LOVETT)

Dear Mistress L.
Yes, Mr T?
Now that it's midnight,
There's just you and me.
Dear Mr T.
Yes, Mistress L?
I should have gone
On the very first bell.
Dear Mistress L.
Yes, Mr T?
Wouldn't you like dear
To sit on my knee?
Dear Mr T.
Yes, Mistress L?
We're not alone
There are others as well.
Dear Mistress L.
Yes, Mr T?
There's but ourselves
As you can't fail to see.
Dear Mr T.
Yes, Mistress L?
It's ghosts of our victims
Tolling our knell.
Dear Mistress L.
Yes, Mr T?

Why don't you stay here
And make love to me?
Dear Mr T.
Yes, Mistress L?
I think I'd rather
See you in - - - -
Oh, Mistress L!
Yes, Mr T?
Surely you couldn't
Wish that on me?
Yes, Mr T!
Oh, Mistress L!
I'm pretty certain
You'd be there as well.

Todd: You are not thinking of going, Mistress Lovett?
Mrs Lovett (*aside*): Twelve o'clock he said at Temple Bar. He will have gone by now. (*Aloud*) It is too late now.
Todd: Why then, let me take your hand again (MRS LOVETT *trembles*) and we will sit here holding hands—like lovers.
Music.

CURTAIN

ACT TWO

SCENE THREE

THE INTERIOR OF MRS LOVETT'S PIE SHOP. *There is a counter stage right covered with trays of pies. Downstage left is a trap door.* MRS LOVETT *is standing centre stage with* JARVIS WILLIAMS *on her right. He is a youth dressed in rags.*

Mrs Lovett: Go away, my dear fellow, go away!

Jarvis: But, mum!

Mrs Lovett: Go away, I say, we never give anything to beggars.

Jarvis: Don't you, mum? I ain't no beggar, mum, but a young man who is on the look out for a situation. I thought as how you might recommend me to some *light* employment where they put the *heavy* work out.

Mrs Lovett: Recommend you!—recommend a ragged wretch like you!

Jarvis: Why bless your innocent heart, mum, it's the conduct, it ain't the toggery that makes the gentleman.

Mrs Lovett: What are you babbling about?

Jarvis: I've seen better days, mum. I kept a vehicle.

Mrs Lovett: I dare say when you get into better case you will have quite sufficient insolence to make you unbearable. Besides, what employment can we have but pie-making? We have a man already who suits us very well, with the exception that he, as you would do if we were to exchange, has grown contemptuous in his calling.

Jarvis: Ah, that is the way of the world. I'll be on my way to seek employment elsewhere. (*Going off right*).

Mrs Lovett (*aside*): If he be unknown he is the very man for our purpose. (*aloud*) Stay! You have solicited employment of me. If I give it to you, you must first furnish me with a reference.

Jarvis: Reference, mum? I haven't got one about me. Maybe this toothpick as I've just found may do. It's real German silver.

"There is blood upon my hands and she is dead!"

SWEENEY TODD *and* MRS LOVETT

"Tell me, boy do you suspect?"

TOBIAS *and* SWEENEY TODD

"I think he will die . . . suddenly."

JONAS FOGG *and* SWEENEY TODD

"You'll never take me—I'll see you in hell first!"

SMITH, MARK *and* SWEENEY TODD

Mrs Lovett: You are ingenuous and I do not see why I should not make a trial of you. Follow me.

Jarvis: Where to?

Mrs Lovett: To the bakehouse, where I will show you what you have to do. But you must make me a promise that you will never leave it on any pretence whatsoever.

Jarvis: Never to leave it!

Mrs Lovett: Never. That is unless to leave it for good and all. If upon those conditions you choose to accept the situation, you may; if not you can depart and leave it alone.

Jarvis: As Shakespeare says, "My poverty and not my will consents". (*She raises a trap door and points below*).

Mrs Lovett: By this passage, young man we must descend to the furnace and ovens, where I will show you how to manufacture the pies, feed the fires and make yourself generally useful.

The lights fade to blackout.

CURTAIN

ACT TWO

SCENE FOUR

THE BAKEHOUSE. *Upstage a backcloth on which is painted a large oven, sacks of flour, etc. Upstage right is a large barrel on which stands a tray of pies. Another barrel is set downstage left and another upstage centre.*

MRS LOVETT *is centre stage when the curtain rises with* JARVIS *to her right looking nervously round the cellar.*

Jarvis : I suppose I am to have someone to assist me in this situation, I swear that one pair of hands could never do the work in such a place.
Mrs Lovett : Are you not content ?
Jarvis : Oh yes. Only you spoke of having a man.
Mrs Lovett (*moving close to* JARVIS) : He has gone to his friends —he has gone to some of his very oldest friends, who will be glad to see him. So now say the word and let me know if you have any scruples.
Jarvis : No, no scruples, but one objection.
Mrs Lovett : And that is ?
Jarvis : I should like to leave when I please.
Mrs Lovett : You may make your mind easy on that score. I can assure you with the greatest degree of truth that I never *keep* anybody many hours after they begin to feel uncomfortable. But now I must leave you a time. As long as you are industrious you will get on very well, but as soon as you begin to get idle and neglect my orders, you will receive a piece of information that may . . .
Jarvis : What is it ? I am of an inquiring disposition; you may as well give it to me now.
Mrs Lovett : No, I seldom find there is occasion for that at first, but after a time, when you get well fed then you are pretty sure to want it. Just heed what I have told you so far and you will not go far amiss (*moves to door right*). And remember, young man, that everybody who relinquishes this situation goes to his old friends—friends that he has not seen for many years. I shall return anon. (*Exit right*).

Jarvis : What a strange manner of talking that respectable middle-aged female has! There seems to be something very singular in all she utters. What the deuce does she mean by a communication being made to me ? It's very strange. And what a singular looking place too—nothing visible but darkness. I think it would be quite unbearable if it wasn't for the delicious odour of the pies. And talking of pies I fancy I could eat one. (*He takes a pie off the tray and sitting on barrel downstage right eats voraciously*) Beautiful! Delicious! Lots of lovely gravy! (*He suddenly discovers a long hair, views it mysteriously and winds it round his finger*).
Somebody's been combing their hair. I don't think that pie's a nice 'un. (*He puts part of eaten pie back and takes another and returns to sit on barrel*).
This is better! Done to a turn! Extremely savoury. (*Puts his hand into his mouth*) What's this—a bone? No, a jacket button! How did a button come into a pie? I don't think I like pies now. Oh la! I'm very poorly! (*Holding his stomach he starts to writhe and groan*) I think I am shortly to die. Oh la! Oh la!

At this moment there is a loud crash from upstage left and JEAN PARMINE *staggers into the room. His clothes are torn and covered with plaster. He is holding an iron bar in his hand.* JARVIS *gets up from the barrel and backs away down right.*

Oh la! Here is one of the murdered ghosts come to ax for his body, what shall I do? Please sir, you can't have it, it's been made into pies. But it wasn't me, sir. I was only engaged today.
Parmine : Silence my friend! You have nothing to fear. I see that, like myself, you have been lured into this den.
Jarvis : Oh, Mr Ghost, sir, I hope that they ain't a-going to murder me as they did you afore me.
Parmine : I am no ghost, never fear. I have escaped the dreadful fate the assassins intended for me and have learnt what became of the unfortunate men who have for some years past disappeared from their families in London, one after the other.
Jarvis : Then you ain't a ghost?

Parmine : Touch me and you will be reassured.

Jarvis (*approaching timidly and then taking a quick jab at* PARMINE): Oh la! It's true you ain't dead!

Parmine : As I told you.

Jarvis : Then sir, since you are flesh and blood and not a ghost, perhaps you can inform me why such a wholesale butchery has been indulged in.

Parmine : The object of the wretches has been entirely robbery, and their victims, people of supposed wealth. They have in all cases been inveigled into the shop of an infamous monster named Sweeney Todd—a barber residing in Fleet Street. At that shop, by an ingenious contrivance, the unfortunate sufferers were lowered to the cellars beneath the house, murdered and conveyed to this retreat, where a glowing furnace destroyed every trace of the crime.

Jarvis : Well, I never! Now I am brought to believe that if anyone had the assistance of the devil in conducting human affairs, I should say, by some means, the parties in question have made it worth the while of his Satanic Majesty to join in the concern.

Parmine : We have no time to lose in idle discourse, but must strike out some plan for our mutual deliverance. Now then, let us first make sure of our correct geographical location. We are in Bell Yard; that much I know to be true, also to my certain knowledge the houses to right and left of us have cellars. Now surely with a weapon such as this bar, willing hearts and arms that have not quite lost their powers, we may make our way from this horrible abode.
(*Noise off*) Hark! Someone is approaching, I must not be seen! Follow me. Leave the matter in my hands, and see if I cannot thwart those who are engaged in this disgusting speculation.

Music. PARMINE *and* JARVIS *exit up left. After a pause,* TODD *enters right and comes downstage centre.*

Todd : Gathering clouds warn the mountaineer of the approaching storm. Let them now warn me to provide against danger. I have too many enemies to be safe. I will dispose of them one by one, till no evidence of my guilt remains, not one single shred, not one iota that can plant the blame onto me. My first step must be to stop the babbling tongue of Tobias Ragg. I need not take his life, for that may be of service to me hereafter, but a close confinement of the boy in the lunatic asylum of Jonas Fogg will effectually silence him. Mistress Lovett now is a different kettle of fish altogether. She grows scrupulous and dissatisfied. I've had an eye on her for some time and fear she intends mischief. A little poison, skilfully administered, may remove any unpleasantness in that quarter. Ha! ha! ha! Who's there? (*He turns suddenly, and discovers* MRS LOVETT *standing at his elbow.*)

Mrs Lovett: Sweeney Todd.

Todd (*calmly*): Well?

Mrs Lovett: Since I discover that you intend treachery I shall on the instant demand my share of the booty, aye, an equal share of the fruits of our mutual bloodshed.

Todd (*with an air of indifference*): Well, you shall have it.

Mrs Lovett: I will have it!

Todd: Will?

Mrs Lovett: Yes, every shilling, every penny!

Todd: Well, so you shall, if you are only patient. I will balance accounts with you in a minute. (*He takes a book from his pocket and runs his fingers down the account*) Twelve thousand pounds to a fraction.

Mrs Lovett: That is just six thousand pounds for each person, there being two of us.

Todd: But Mistress Lovett, I must first have you to know that before I hand you a coin, you will have to pay me for your support, lodging and clothes.

Mrs Lovett: Clothes?

Todd: I repeat the word—clothes!

Mrs Lovett: Why, I haven't had a dress for these six months.

Todd: Besides, am I to have nothing for your education? (*Draws his fingers significantly across his throat*) Yes, for some years you have been totally provided for by me, and after deducting that and the expenses of erecting furnaces, purchasing flour for your delicious pies, etc., etc., I find it leaves a balance of sixteen shillings and fourpence three farthings in my favour. And I do not intend you to budge an inch until it has been paid.

Mrs Lovett : You want to rob me, but you shall find to your sorrow, I will have my due. (*She secretly draws a knife, her hand is raised against* TODD, *who confronts her.* TODD *starts back on seeing the weapon*). Now, villain, who triumphs ? I have the whip hand now and you will dance to my tune. Put your name to a deed consigning the whole of the wealth that blood has purchased, or you perish where you stand!

Todd : Idiot! (*Aside*) She should have known Sweeney Todd better and learnt that he is a man to calculate his chances. (*Aloud*) Behold! (*He draws a pistol from his pocket*) Now say your prayers, your last hour has come! (*He takes the knife from her hand.* MRS LOVETT *throws herself at his feet*).

Mrs Lovett : Spare my life, for the love of Heaven, as I spared yours. You cannot have the heart to kill me. (*Clinging to him*) I will not loose my hold, you cannot throw me off. Oh stop before you spill my blood. I have been true to you. I swear it upon my guilty soul.

Todd : Off! off!

Music.

Mrs Lovett : The good lady and gentleman told me of a home where I could end my days in solitude and peace. Let me see them again and beg them on my knees to show the same mercy and compassion unto you—let us never see each other more, let us lead better lives and forget we ever lived except in prayer.

Todd : You will not loose your hold ? (*He brandishes the knife*).

Mrs Lovett : It is never too late to repent, never . . .

Todd : Perdition! (*He stabs her and then stands motionless for a moment. Then he moves to centre stage as the whole of the stage is plunged into red light*) There is blood upon my hands, and she is dead . . . dead! dead! Now, let the furnace consume the body, as it would wheaten straw, and destroy all evidence of my guilt in this, as it has in my manifold deeds of blood.

CURTAIN

ACT THREE

SCENE ONE

SWEENEY TODD'S SHOP. *When the curtain rises* TOBIAS *is seated in the chair right looking miserable.*

Tobias: How unhappy I am here. I fear that something terrible will happen to me. How I wish I was at home with my dear mother. I wonder if she thinks of me today? I know I think of her all the time and today especially for—
He sings:

IT'S MY MOTHER'S BIRTHDAY

(TOBIAS)

REFRAIN I

It's my mother's birthday and I mustn't forget.
It's my mother's birthday and I'm her little pet.
I will choose a gift for her
To fill her heart with joy,
For it's my mother's birthday
And I'm her favourite boy.

(*Rises from chair to centre stage*)

VERSE I

Mothers are sweet and kind,
Mothers are good and true,
And you will always find,
They'll work and slave for you   and . . .

REFRAIN II

It's my mother's birthday, her very own day.
It's my mother's birthday, her hair is turning grey,
She was young and sweet and fair,
But time has shown his hand,
But on my mother's birthday,
She's fairest in the land.

VERSE II

Mothers are pure as gold,
Mothers will calm your fear,
Close in their arms they'll hold
Those that they love most dear   and . . .

REFRAIN III

It's my mother's birthday and I want her to know,
On my mother's birthday that I do love her so.
I'm as poor as poor can be,
My gift will be but small,
But on my mother's birthday,
She'll like it best of all.

At the end of the song JARVIS *rushes on from right.*

Jarvis : At last, Tobias, I fancy I have got to the bottom of the mystery. This house communicates with next door and in it Sweeney Todd hides his victims until he gets rid of them in the shape of his juicy confectionery—pies, all hot! By touching a spring in the mantlepiece, the opening to Lovett's house is discovered, but it is difficult for one person to remove on his own. I don't think I need to ask if you will lend me a hand?

Tobias : I will indeed, most certainly. But we must use caution in the proceeding and await our opportunity. Most likely tomorrow I shall be able to frame some excuse by which I may get Sweeney Todd out of the way, and we shall have plenty of time to make the venture. At present it would be dangerous, as I expect his return every minute.

Jarvis : Then I'll make myself scarce at once (*moves up right*).

Tobias : Hush! I hear footsteps.

Jarvis (*turning*) : Talk of the devil and he's at your elbow. I wonder how he'd eat in one of his own pies? (*He goes out up right*).

After a moment TODD *enters hurriedly, he looks suspiciously and attentively at* TOBIAS, *who stares at him in fear.*

Todd : And what are you staring at, boy?

Tobias : I wasn't staring, sir.

Todd : Don't be impertinent! (*to right of* TOBIAS) Now tell me what you are doing?

Tobias : Nothing.

Todd : Then finish the job at once, and begin something else.

Tobias : Shall I put away the casket you have in your hand?

A glance between TODD *and* TOBIAS *then* TODD *strikes him and he falls down right.*

Todd : There's a lesson for you to learn. It will teach you to make no remarks about what don't concern you. You may think whatever you like but you shall only say what *I* like, Tobias Ragg.

Tobias (*getting to his feet*) : I won't endure it! I won't be knocked about in this way, I won't.

Todd : You won't eh? Ha! ha! heugh! Have you forgotten your mother?

Tobias : You say that you have power over my mother, but I don't know what it is and I cannot and will not believe it. I'll leave you, come of it what may. (*Runs across to door right*) I'll go to sea. I'll go anywhere rather than stay in such a place as this.

Todd : Oh, you will, will you? (*moving to* TOBIAS) Then let me tell you, Tobias Ragg, that you and I must come to some understanding. I'll tell you what power I have over your mother and then perhaps you'll be satisfied.

Tobias : I am persuaded that while I live to protect her you can do her no injury.

Todd : Then, shall I tell you, Tobias, eh? Shall I tell you what is the power as you call it that I have over your dear mother?.

Tobias : As you will, Mr Todd.

Todd : Do you remember last winter, Tobias, eh, do you remember it?

Music.

Tobias : I do of certainty, Mr Todd, it was a very cold winter.

Todd : It was indeed, cruel cold. As I recall it the frost continued for eighteen weeks and you, Tobias, you were starving. Your mother, Mrs Ragg, was employed to attend the chambers of a lawyer in the Temple. He was a cold-hearted severe man, who never forgave anything in his life and who you can be sure never will.

Tobias : The home was indeed desolate. A guinea was owing for rent but mother got the money, paid it, and obtained the situation where she is now.

Todd : Ah, you think so. The rent was paid, but, Tobias my boy, a word in your ear, she took a candlestick from her employer to pay it.

Music ends.

Tobias : It's not true! You lie in an attempt to hold me here. My mother is a good woman, good and kind, never would she do anyone a disservice, or be guilty of a dishonest act.

Todd : I know it! And what is more I can prove it. And I will hang her if you force me by your conduct (*moves upstage laughing*).

Tobias : Liar and calumniator! It is time you should know with whom you have to deal. This infamous charge against an innocent woman has given me a nerve of iron. I utterly throw off the yoke imposed by you upon me and . . . (*runs to door right*).

Todd (*to door—blocking exit*) : Where are you going ?

Tobias : To the nearest magistrate. There I will denounce Sweeney Todd and deliver into the hands of justice a designing, cruel and cold-blooded murderer.

Todd : Tobias Ragg, you have pronounced your doom!

A desperate struggle takes place between TOBIAS *and* TODD. *After a frantic chase around the stage in which the chairs are overturned,* TOBIAS *is overpowered and the razor of* TODD *is raised as the centre chair sinks and rises again with* MARK INGESTRE *seated in it. At the same time the stage lighting fades and the chair is covered with a green light.* TODD *stares at him in horror. This picture is held for a moment.*

Todd (*backing away*) : Ah! The yawning grave yields up its ghastly inmate to fix my guilt! Blood will have blood! See he is there. There he comes to accuse me of the murder. Save me! Save me! I swear 'twas not I that slew him. I swear it. Let me hence, or it will kill me. Ha! ha! ha!

He laughs hysterically as the

CURTAIN FALLS

ACT THREE

SCENE 2

A CHAMBER IN THE MADHOUSE AT PECKHAM. *There is a table centre stage with a chair above it and another to the left of it. On the table is a ledger and a large hand bell. A clock strikes five as* JONAS FOGG, *the keeper of the madhouse enters from down left and limps up to the table.*

Fogg : Five o'clock and not arrived. Mr Todd is late; he is generally a very punctual man. (*He sits in the chair above the table and consults the ledger*) Let me see P, Q, R, S, T,—Todd, Fleet Street, London. Paid one year's keep and burial of Thomas Simkins, aged fifteen, found dead in his bed, after a residence in the asylum of ten months and four days. I think that was our last transaction. Some of our patients do die very suddenly, and somehow or other we never know how it happens. It must be some sort of a fit, for they are found dead in the morning in their beds. Then I bury them quietly and privately without anyone knowing the slightest thing about it. (*Knock at door*) 'Tis he, I said he was a very punctual man (*rises and moves to door right*).

TODD *enters right and crosses to centre stage.*

Fogg (*moving to* TODD) : Mr Sweeney Todd, I think, if my memory don't deceive me.

Todd : You are right, Mr Jonas Fogg, I believe I am not easily forgotten by those who have once seen me.

Fogg (*with great point*) : True, sir. You are not easily forgotten. Pray be seated, Mr Todd. (TODD *sits left of table,* FOGG *above*) What can I do for you this time, sir ?

Todd : I am more than a little worried, Mr Fogg, I seem to be rather unfortunate with my boys. I treat them with utmost care and I lavish affection upon them as I might do if I was their very own father. But in spite of my loving attentions I am, as I say, most unfortunate.

Fogg : What would the trouble be this time, Mr Todd.

Todd : As before, Mr Fogg, as before. I have got another one here who has shown such decided symptoms of insanity, that it becomes, I regret to say, absolutely necessary to place him under your care.

Fogg : Indeed, but first let me know the symptoms. (*Taking up a pen to write in ledger*) Does he rave?

Todd : Oh yes, he does, and about the most absurd nonsense in the world. In fact to hear him one would think that instead of being one of the most humane of men I was, in point of fact, an absolute murderer.

Fogg : A murderer?

Todd : Yes, a murderer, to all intents and purposes a murderer. I ask you, Mr Fogg, could anything in the world be more absurd than such an accusation? I, Sweeney Todd, who have the milk of human kindness flowing in every vein, who would not harm a single hair of the meanest of God's creatures.

Fogg : Quite, quite.

Todd : I, who would stoop to help the lame dog over the stile. Why my very appearance ought to be sufficient to convince anybody at once of my sweet and considerate disposition.

Fogg : As you say, Mr Todd. Absurd that any person could mistake the sort of man you really are.

Todd : Exactly.

Fogg : Now as to the boy, Mr Todd, for how long do you think this malady will continue?

Todd (*rising and moving away left*) : I will pay for twelve months, but I do not think between you and I, that the case will last anything like so long.

Fogg : You think not, Mr Todd?

Todd (*turning*) : I am almost certain of it, Mr Fogg. (*Up to* FOGG *and putting his face close to* FOGG's) I think that he will die like Simkins . . . suddenly.

Fogg : I shouldn't wonder if he did.

Todd (*moving away up left*) : It is decidedly the best way, because it saves a great deal of trouble and annoyance to friends and relations, as well as preventing expense, which might otherwise be foolishly gone into.

Fogg : We make no remarks, and we ask no questions. Those are the principles on which we have conducted this establishment so successfully and so long. Those are the principles on which we shall continue to conduct it, and to merit, we hope the patronage of the public.

Todd: Unquestionably, most unquestionably.

Fogg: You may as well introduce me to your patient at once. I suppose by this time he has been brought into the house?

Todd: Certainly, I shall have great pleasure in showing him to you (*going to door*) Tobias Ragg, come into the room directly. Tobias Ragg!!

There is no response—TODD *goes off right and bundles* TOBIAS *into the room.* FOGG *rises and moves downstage to stand left of* TOBIAS *who is on* TODD'S *left.*

Fogg (*with mock concern*): This is the lad?

Todd (*in a similar tone*): This is he, poor, poor, boy.

Fogg: Quite young.

Todd: Yes, more's the pity, and of course we deeply lament his present position.

Fogg: Of course, but see . . . he raises his eyes. (TOBIAS *fixes a glance on* TODD) He will speak directly.

Todd (*violently*): Rave you mean, don't call it speaking, it's not entitled to the name. Hush! Listen!

Tobias: Sweeney Todd is a murderer, a foul murderer and I denounce him.

Todd: You hear him? Did I not tell you?

Fogg: Mad indeed!

Tobias (*catching hold of* FOGG, *pleadingly*): Oh save me, save me from this foul monster. It is my life he seeks because I know his dreadful secret. He is a murderer, a cruel murderer, I tell you!

Todd: You see?

Fogg: Indeed, yes.

Tobias: Listen to me I implore you. Save me from the clutches of this inhuman butcher. Ask him, ask him, what happens to the persons who come into his shop and who never leave it again in life.

Todd: Could anyone but a maniac make so absurd an assertion?

Fogg: No, it is insanity in its most terrible form. I shall be under the necessity of putting him in a strait-waistcoat (*pushing* TOBIAS *away to down right*).

Todd: As you think fit, Mr Fogg. I am afraid that mild treatment which I have tried only irritates the disease. Therefore I must leave you as a professional man, to deal with the case as your experience tells you necessary. But time presses and I have an important engagement to fulfil and so must wish you good day, Mr Fogg. I have no doubt whatsoever that the patient will be properly attended to. (*Shakes hands with* FOGG *and moves down to* TOBIAS) Ha! ha! How do you feel now, Tobias? Do you think I shall hang or will you die in the cell of a madhouse?

Exit TODD *laughing.*

Tobias (*moving up to* FOGG *and kneeling*): I don't know who you are, sir, or where I am, but let me beg of you to have the house of Sweeney Todd, in Fleet Street, searched, and you will find proof beyond all doubt that he is indeed a murderer. There are at least a hundred watches, rings and trinkets, all belonging to the unfortunate persons who from time to time have met their death through him.

Fogg: How uncommonly mad!

Tobias (*rising*): No, no, indeed I am not mad. Why call me so when the truth or falsehood of what I say can be so easily ascertained. Search his house and if those things are not found, then say I am mad and have but dreamt of them. I do not know how he kills people, that is a great mystery to me, but that he does kill them I have no doubt—I cannot have a doubt.

FOGG *moves up to table and rings bell loudly—a keeper enters right.*

Fogg: You will take this lad under your care as he seems extremely feverish and unsettled. Shave his head and put a strait-waistcoat on him. Let him be conveyed to one of the dark, damp cells as too much light encourages his wild delirium.

Keeper: Come along with me boy (*catches hold of him roughly*).

Tobias: Oh no! no! What have I done that I should be

subjected to such cruel treatment? What have I done that I should be placed in a cell? If this be a madhouse, I am not mad—oh, have mercy on me!

Fogg: Give him nothing but bread and water.

Tobias: No! no! Have pity on me!

Fogg: The first symptoms of his recovery which will produce better treatment will be his exonerating his master from what he said about him, for he must be mad as long as he continues to accuse a kind gentleman like Mr Todd of such things.

Tobias: Then I shall continue mad, for if it be madness to know and aver that Sweeney Todd is an assassin, mad I am for it is true.

Fogg: Take him away, I swear he is more vicious than any patient we have had here for a considerable time.

Keeper: Come along you.

Tobias: I will die ere I submit to you and your vile thugs.

Fogg: Then die, for no power can aid you! (*moving away upstage left*).

Tobias: Yes, there is one!(*points upwards*) Heaven which fails not to succour the helpless and persecuted. *He sings:*

HEAVEN

(TOBIAS)

REFRAIN I

Heaven, Heaven, Heaven will answer my prayer.
Never, never, never have I need to care.
Courage, courage, courage to stand the test.
I am but a feeble lad,
And Heaven alone knows best.

VERSE I

Unhappy am I, unhappy and sad.
Gone are the plans for my future I had.
All of my hopes are driven away,
Oh what a terrible, miserable day but . . .

REFRAIN II

Heaven, Heaven, Heaven will come to my aid.
Never, never, never must I be afraid,

Sunshine, sunshine, sunshine will follow the rain.
So I'll pray to Heaven above
To give me my freedom again.

VERSE II

Why has cruel fate decreed this to be?
What have I done that this happened to me?
They will not listen, they think me insane,
I fear that I'll ne'er see blue skies again but . . .

REFRAIN III

Heaven, Heaven, Heaven won't fail me at all,
Ever, ever, ever will they hear my call.
Angels, angels, angels will watch over me,
And I know that Heaven above,
Will see that at last I'm set free.

Heaven will aid me—fear not!

As FOGG *and the* KEEPER *advance to seize* TOBIAS *there is a loud crash of glass up left and* JARVIS WILLIAMS *dashes in and protecting* TOBIAS, *confronts the others with his fists—the picture is held for a moment.*

Jarvis: Stand off you cowardly rascals, or I'll put the 'kiebosh' on the whole 'consarn.'

Fogg: The 'kiebosh'?

Jarvis: Yes, it's a word of Greek extraction, signifying the upset of the apple cart—so—bunk.

Fogg: Bunk?

Jarvis: Yes, that's another Greek word and means G.O. GO!

Fogg: Not if we know it.

Jarvis: You won't?

Fogg: No!

Jarvis: Then, damn me if I don't make you. Tobias assist me and we'll lock up these rascals in their own madhouse.

*Music—*JARVIS *seizes* FOGG *by the throat and* TOBIAS *attacks the* KEEPER. *In no time at all the men are spreadeagled on the floor with* TOBIAS *and* JARVIS *sitting on them. They sing:*

HEAVEN (Reprise)

(TOBIAS AND JARVIS)

Heaven, Heaven, Heaven has answered our prayer.
Never, never, never had we need to care.
Sunshine, sunshine, sunshine has followed the rain.
We have prayed to Heaven above
And Heaven has answered our prayer.

On the last line of the song JARVIS *and* TOBIAS *raise their eyes and arms to above and the stage lighting comes up to its maximum.*

CURTAIN

ACT THREE

SCENE THREE

TEMPLE STAIRS. *There is a bench right centre and part of a wall and a lamp standard left. It is moonlight.* COLONEL JEFFREY *is walking up and down.*

Jeffrey: Johanna will be true to her appointment, I have no doubt, though I have little to make known to her with respect to her missing lover. 'Tis strange since our last interview, a feeling to which I have been hitherto a stranger should have assailed me. (*He moves down left*) Is it possible—could it be love? Yes, if Mark Ingestre be dead, there is no dishonour in the acknowldgement and a beautiful girl is not to be shut out from the pale of all affection because the first person to whom her heart has warmed is no more.

Enter JOHANNA *from right.*

(*Turns*) Ah, she is here! Your servant, Miss Oakley. I rejoice again to meet you.

Johanna: Pardon me, sir, if I dispense with all the common observances of courtesy, as my mind is ill at ease. Tell me, I pray you, at once if you bring sad or gladsome tidings.

Jeffrey: I have heard nothing, my good young lady, that can give you satisfaction concerning the fate of Mark Ingestre, but I have suspicion that something serious must have indeed happened to him.

Johanna: I do sincerely hope from my heart that such a suspicion may be dissipated. I hope it because I tell you freely and frankly, dim and obscure as the hope is, that I believe that Mark has escaped the murderous hands raised against him.

Jeffrey: Believe me, my dear Miss Oakley, if the sacrifice of my life would be a relief—if it could in any way save you from the pain you suffer, then it would, I assure you, be sacrificed most willingly.

Johanna: No! No! Heaven knows enough has been sacrificed already—more than enough—much more than enough. But do not suppose that I am ungrateful for the generous interest you have taken in me. No, believe me, Colonel Jeffrey, among the few names that are enrolled in my breast, and such to me will ever be honoured—remember, yours will be found while I live. But that I fear will not be for very much longer.

Jeffrey: Do not speak despairingly.

Johanna: Have I not cause for despair?

Jeffrey: You have cause for grief but scarcely for despair.

Johanna: I will ascertain the fate of Mark Ingestre or perish.

Jeffrey: You alarm me by those words, as well as by your manner of uttering them. Let me implore you to be careful of yourself and not to risk much in order that perhaps you may have some remote chance of achieving very little. I entreat you to leave the task to me of what attempts may be made to discover your lover's destiny. There must be danger in even enquiring for him, if there has been any foul play—and therefore I ask you to let that danger be mine alone.

Johanna: I will accord with your wishes thus far, and promise that I will attempt nothing that shall not have the possibility of success attending it. Return here tomorrow at the same hour and I will divulge to you the scheme I have in view with regard to this terrible mystery.

Jeffrey: As you will, Miss Oakley, I will attend you at this hour tomorrow. And so farewell, and do not let despair o'ertake you.

Johanna: Farewell, good kind friend. (*Exit*).

Jeffrey (*moving down left*): I love her, but she seems in no respect willing to enchain her heart. Alas! how sad it is for me, that the woman who above all others I could wish to call my own, instead of being a joy to me, I have only encountered that she might impart a pang to my soul. Beautiful and excellent Johanna I love you, but I see that your affections are withered for ever.

Enter TODD *in a mask and cloak. He goes to right of* JEFFREY.

Todd: Unless I am much mistaken I address myself to Colonel Jeffrey.

Jeffrey: That is indeed my name, sir, may I enquire what yours may be?

Todd: That is of no consequence, sir, let us say that I am your friend—a man who has your safety much to heart.

Jeffrey: What do you mean?

Todd: Colonel Jeffrey you are in danger—terrible danger.

Jeffrey: Indeed! From whom may I ask?

Todd: Follow me and you will soon find out your enemy.

He moves across to right with appropriate music.

Jeffrey: Wait, sir, I must first know who and what you are before I consent to be guided by a man who disguises his features by wearing a mask.

Todd (*checking*): I wear this mask for other purposes than concealment, which it is not judicious to explain at the present moment.

Jeffrey: Unless you are more explicit I cannot, I consider with safety to myself, consent to accompany you. I ask you again what is your name?

Todd (*moving across to* JEFFREY): And I repeat to you my assurance that I am a man friendly disposed towards you.

Jeffrey: Nevertheless, this assertion still fails to move my scruples.

Todd: Why should it do so? But since you distrust me I must leave, and you will remain without the information I was about to afford. (*He moves right again--Music*).

Jeffrey (*aside*): Can it be? I am in doubt and fear how to act in this most strange intercourse—(*aloud*) Stay my friend, since you say you are a friend to me, have you no token by which I may recognise amity?

Todd: That I have—an undeniable one! (*He produces the pearls from beneath his cloak and holds them up—Music*).

Jeffrey: Great Heavens! The string of pearls!

Todd: Yes, the string of pearls indeed (*pushes them into* JEFFREY'S *hand*).

Jeffrey: Who are you, sir, and how came these pearls into your possession? Answer me for I must know without any further delay. This matter is one of the greatest urgency.

Todd: Hasten with me to the shop of Sweeney Todd, the Barber of Fleet Street and you will there learn who and what

I am, and more of the the owner of the gems than I can tell you here.

Jeffrey : Say you so? Then I have tarried too long, my impatience to fathom the mystery is so great that I wish our onward speed could leave the wind behind us. Come, let us no further time be lost by discourse. (*He rushes out right*).

Todd (*centre stage*) : So! He has the pearls in his possession—good! I can now denounce him, and remove the grave suspicion that attaches itself to the name of Sweeney Todd. (*Exit*).

Music.

Enter DR LUPIN. JARVIS WILLIAMS *comes on slowly behind him.*

Lupin (*moving down right—aside*) : Verily, hypocrisy is the ladder by which to mount. From the very lowest rung did I begin, then slowly did I ascend—step by step until I reached the topmost. It hath made a man of me, and that carcase which was as lank as a herring is now round and comely to look upon. Ah, 'tis a sinful world, a sinful world indeed!

Jarvis (*aside*) : That's my man sure enough. Now to treat him with a surprise he little expects (*he creeps up behind* LUPIN *and slaps him on the back*) Hullo, my Tulip!

Lupin (*starting*) : Avaunt—of a verity my name is Lupin.

Jarvis : Any fool knows a tulip and a lupin ain't the same plant. You're a rum 'un you are.

Lupin : Rum! Peradventure I may have partaken of that carnal fluid in a cup of tea with the pious dame who vends the article at yonder sinful public-house, but for medicinal purposes only, for spasms sorely afflict this rebellious stomach of mine.

Jarvis : I want a word with you since I see you are of a sanctimonious turn.

Lupin : I despise not the ungodly, that I may teach them the errors of their ways, but I may not like thy company for . . .

Jarvis : I see you are not comfortable in the company of respectable people.

Lupin : Thy wit is thrown away.

Jarvis : It generally is on a fool.

Lupin : Fool! Thou knowest me not!

Jarvis: Not I! Who the devil are you?
Lupin: I am an honest man.
Jarvis: How folks are deceived by appearances! You look for all the world like a rogue (*he moves away right*).
Lupin (*aside*): I like not this unseemly fellow. The spirit moveth me to depart—I will gird up my loins and flee (*he starts to go off right*).
Jarvis: Stop! Stop! I've not done with you yet, old sobersides. I've a few more questions to ax. Were you ever in the West Indies?
Lupin: Yes—that is—no!
Jarvis: Yes—no? Mind what you are about, Mr Honest Man, or you'll get into hot water. I say again, were you ever in the West Indies?
Lupin: Why askest thou?
Jarvis (*moving to exit and pointing off stage*): Because here is a black woman and five black children that claim some relationship. (*Exit*).
Lupin (*running across right to look off and then backing away in consternation*): My wife, Cloe, by all that's damnable! (*He rushes off left as the lights fade to blackout*).

CURTAIN

ACT THREE

SCENE FOUR

A COURT OF JUSTICE. *A large window dominates the back of the stage. In front of it is seated the Judge,* SIR WILLIAM BRANDON. *To the left of him is the witness box and below it and to the left the dock in which stands the prisoner,* COLONEL JEFFREY.

On stage right are benches on which are seated members of the public who interrupt the proceedings loudly throughout the trial. Below right of the Judge stands the COURT USHER.

Judge: That the prisoner at the bar is either an accomplice in the murder of the unfortunate man, or the actual perpetrator of the deed, there is strong evidence. His absence from his home without any special reason and the discovery of the pearls on his person can lead to no other supposition than he must be in some way connected with the mysterious affair upon which we are adjudicating. What your motive was, prisoner, can be clearly conceived—your victim was the only bar between you and the object of your affection, Johanna Oakley.

Jeffrey: My Lord, circumstances are against me. I can make no defence, can call no witness to prove my innocence—the stranger from whom I received those pearls has failed to make his appearance, and my bare word is nothing . . .

Judge: The statement that you received these pearls from an unknown person in a public thoroughfare is so improbable that it cannot for a moment be accepted as truth.

Jeffrey: Then I must sink into the grave with ignominy, and my name, which has hitherto been untarnished by dishonour, become the scorn of all honest men.

Judge: The only chance of life left you, prisoner, hangs on this mysterious letter, but its purpose is so vague that I cannot offer you any hope on that score (*reads letter*). 'Let the hand of justice for a moment be arrested, ere sentence is pronounced a witness will appear and confound the guilty in their hour of triumph.' I have to tell you that that witness has not appeared and there remains but one other to examine. Let him stand forth.

Usher: Sweeney Todd! Sweeney Todd!

TODD *enters up left and goes into witness box.*

Jeffrey: I protest, my Lord. You will not take the evidence of this man. A man who . . .

Judge: Silence! Witness, make your deposition.

Todd: My Lord, I cannot but express my deep regret at being called to testify against one who has held the good opinion of the world, but duty and justice compel me to speak. I had taken into my service a fatherless lad named Tobias Ragg . . .

Judge: One moment! This boy, having been taken into your service has been stated in the earlier stages of the trial. Is that boy here?

Todd: No, my Lord! Since the murder of Mark Ingestre, he can be found nowhere, though a most diligent search has been made by the officers. It is supposed that, being an accomplice of the prisoner, he has . . .

Jeffrey: My Lord, surely the unsupported testimony of this designing man will not be suffered to condemn me and . . .

Judge: This interruption augers ill for your judgement, prisoner. You will have an opportunity of replying in due season, and receive every advantage justice can yield. Witness, proceed with your attestation.

A green light burns at the gauze window, and the form of MARK INGESTRE *appears for an instant.* TODD *stands transfixed.*

Todd: 'Twas his form—I saw it distinctly! Can the dead rise from the grave?

Judge: Why do you pause, witness? The court is waiting to hear the rest of your deposition.

Todd: My Lord, it is impossible that I can give evidence while that figure is gleaming upon me from yonder window. (MARK INGESTRE *vanishes*). Gone!—'twas but the picture of a distraught brain. Your pardon, my Lord—a sudden giddiness, nothing more.

Judge: Then we will proceed. Let the string of pearls be produced. (*The* USHER *takes the pearls across to* TODD). Show them to the witness. (*They are given to* TODD) These are the same pearls that it has been stated were taken from the murdered man. Now, witness, can you swear to them?

Todd (*examining them*): Without a shadow of doubt, my Lord. These are the very pearls.

Judge: Can you tell us why you can recognise them with such certainty?

Todd: Yes, the clasp is so curiously and cleverly devised you might distinguish it among a thousand others. (*Hands back pearls to* USHER *who returns right*).

Judge: And you have seen it in the possession of Mark Ingestre?

Todd: Have I seen it in his possession? Shame, shame—why do you ask such a question? Do you not see him coming to claim it? Ask him, I say, he is coming towards the judgement seat. (*The figure of* MARK INGESTRE *appears beside* JUDGE *in a red spot*). Look, my Lord Judge, Mark Ingestre is by your side! Do not whisper to him. Your ermined robe is stained with blood—stained with blood!—blood!—blood! Ha! ha! ha! (*The figure again vanishes*).

Judge: What is this? Witness, your words are incoherent and wild. Your frantic gesture would lead us to suppose that reason has resigned her throne to mad despair. If your nerves are unstrung by the painful office you undertake, then you have the permission of this court to retire awhile so that you may recover your self-possession.

Todd: Yes, it was a dark foul deed, but heed not what you hear, Lord Judge—the prisoner has brought his victim! What! Do you still remain and suffer such corruptness? I feared it would come to this and through accursed gold—for which men sell their souls and barter their eternal salvation! (*The figure of* MARK INGESTRE *stands beside* TODD *in the witness box —the lights fade except for a blue spot on* MARK *and* TODD). Ha! ha! I am undone—all is lost. Keep away from me, keep away! It is useless to deny my guilt. The very dead rise from their graves to prove that I, Sweeney Todd, am a murderer—a murderer! (*He falls*).

CURTAIN

ACT FOUR

SCENE ONE

THE ENTRANCE TO NEWGATE PRISON. *Centre stage are the gates leading to the prison. There is a table down left on which are set bottles, glasses and tankards. Seated behind the table is* MRS POORLEAN, *a large, fat woman. Two warders are standing right. Three or four idlers are waiting the opportunity of seeing the new prisoner,* SWEENEY TODD.

1st Bystander: Where is he? What have they done with the murderer?

2nd Bystander: How much longer must we wait to see the villain?

3rd Bystander: They say he is the foulest creature ever created.

2nd Bystander: Evil-looking he is too, in truth.

1st Bystander: I swear that when I set eyes on him I shall faint away.

1st Warder: Sorry to keep you waiting, ladies and gentlemen, Sweeney Todd will be moving shortly.

Enter LUPIN *from right.*

Lupin (*to* WARDERS): Brethren, I am told that in this den of thieves you have a wondrous expert fellow worth the seeing. Canst thou oblige me?

1st Warder: Have you any business with him?

Lupin: That I have; verily my business is to rebuke him. My spirit is full of exhortations.

1st Warder: Why then, let your heart be full of generosity or he'll laugh at you and your exhortations too. If you'll contribute something in charity towards his upkeep, give it to me and I'll pass it on.

Lupin: Verily I would give anything to save his soul, but for his body I can give no more than a sixpenny piece.

1st Warder: Well, every little helps (*pockets sixpence*). You must wait here. (*A sound of the rattle of chains off, and prisoners singing*):

HERE IN THE JUG
(CHORUS)

Here in the jug, hopeless we lie,
Sent by the beak for to rot and to die.
Strong are our chains, black is our woe,
Off to the hangman soon we must go.

2nd Warder: Note the free entertainment we give you, ladies and gentlemen.

Me and my 'dolly' pals in the box,
We've got a plan the gaolers to fox,
When they come round at the end of the day,
All of the lags will have broken away.

1st Warder: I am not pleased with the sentiment of that song. It seems to smack of danger. (*Exit*).
Lupin (*aside*): I find that my outward man, after so much psalm singing, wanteth refreshment. I will therefore confabulate with that well-grown damsel (*moving to right of table*). (*Aloud*) Wife, virgin, thou hast an abundance of oil in thy lamp if I am not mistaken. The morning being cold I would willingly qualify it with something comforting and refreshing. What hast thou got?
Mrs Poorlean: Sir, because you are a friend, I will entertain you with my favourite bottle (*pours him a generous measure*). Hey—drink up and let us converse a while.
Lupin (*drinks*): Ah—in truth 'tis excellent, very excellent. (*She refills his glass*) Thank you good woman. Pray, tell me do the frogs of this lake of darkness regail with such choice liquors?
Mrs Poorlean: Some of the better sort that can afford it do, but they are for the generality such poor rogues—my service to you.
Lupin: Thou needest not say that; thy love is enough. (*Aside*) Verily this creature warmeth. (*Drinks*) Verily thou art as round as a full moon and as fleshy as the goats that wanton on the delectable mountain. Thy tabernacle is full with mammon. Hast thou not an idol in thy inward woman to

whom thou sacrificest day and night, as of old the heathen gave up their babes to be devoured by Moloch?

Mrs Poorlean: Ha! ha! You are a comical gent. No, no, mine is nothing but sheer fat. You may feel it if you please.

LUPIN *slyly iabs her stomach.*

Lupin: Verily you speak truth, 'tis fat indeed. (*Aside*) Verily flesh is prevailing. (*Aloud*) Woman I shall come and see thee pretty often. But no more now; we may be observed by the profane.

2nd Warder: Well, ladies and gentlemen, if you will follow me I can now take you to see this famous prisoner, Sweeney Todd, in his cell. Follow me, please.

2nd Bystander: Now to see the monster safely behind bars.

1st Bystander: If he is not I swear I shall faint away.

2nd Warder: Come along now if you have a mind to see him.

Re-enter FIRST WARDER *running across the stage.*

1st Warder: Hi! hi! Lockfast! Lockfast! Come here at once.

2nd Warder: What's happened—what's amiss?

1st Warder: The bird is flown, Todd is gone.

2nd Warder: Gone?

1st Warder: Yes, he's escaped his cell. Hi! hi! Tell the Governor! Ring the bells!

2nd Bystander: Let us depart from here in haste, the villain's abroad. (*Exit*).

1st Bystander: I shall faint, I know I shall faint if I so much as set eyes on him. (*Exit*).

3rd Bystander: Quick—let us be gone. (*Exit*).

The prison bell starts to toll.

Mrs Poorlean: I like this not, I'm off at speed. (*She runs off*).

Lupin (*alone on stage*): Verily he is fled. He is gone like the flower of the field and the flower fadeth and the man vanisheth and then shall be said in those days, 'Woe to England for

Todd is escaped! Woe, woe, woe, for the roaring lion is abroad and no throats shall remain of a piece'. Oh that my head were a fountain of water, running pure milk to weep salt tears for the crying sins of this nation. (*He starts to go off right and then checks centre stage*). Milk! (*He returns to the table, looks round to see that he is not observed, picks up a bottle and walks off right slowly with the air of a righteous man*). Milk! Milk!

Music.

CURTAIN

ACT FOUR

SCENE TWO

THE BAKEHOUSE. *The body of* MRS LOVETT *is lying centre stage.* SWEENEY TODD *is alone—he is pale and distraught. A thunderstorm is heard throughout the following scene.*

Todd: I think I have given them the slip now—but I am weary and would fain rest awhile (*sits on barrel down right centre*). What happened? I am so weary that my brain is fuddled and refuses to impart to me its knowledge. Let me think awhile. Ah, yes, I remember now, they were crying after me down Ludgate Hill—I ran—straight and swift I ran, and no one dare to stop me. I heard the noise of feet behind and redoubled my speed. It grew fainter and fainter in the distance and at length died away altogether, but on I bounded, through marsh and rivulet, over fence and wall, with a wild shout which was taken up by the strange beings that flocked around me on every side, swelling the sound till it pierced the air. I was borne upon the arms of demons who swept along upon the wind and bore down bank and hedge before them, and spun me round and round with a rustle and a speed that made my head swim, until at last they threw me from them with a violent shock and I fell heavily upon the earth.
. . . And then I woke and crawled back here. What was it I came for? My head aches. I cannot remember. I cannot remember (*rising and moving down stage left*). But I must, I must, 'twas for a matter of great import—that I can recall—what was it?—Now I mix up realities with my dreams and having so much to do, and always being hurried hither and thither, have no time to separate the two from some strange confusion in which they get involved. . . . I remember now—it was money—and some jewels—but not here. Yes, the money was here. (*Moving down right and picking up a cash box which he shakes and puts back where he found it*) And the jewels—oh, my poor head. Have I forgotten where I hid them? Was it in the shop? What's that? Footsteps. I can hear footsteps on the stairs. (*Moving to door right and shouting*) You can't come

down those stairs. Only Mistress Lovett and Sweeney Todd know of those stairs and that Smith. But he's dead. Go away! You can't come down here! Go away, I say! Go away! . . . Quietly, quietly—it was only the wind. (*Moves about the cellar*) Ah—here you are Mistress Lovett. Somebody's cut your throat. Tell me who did it. Tell Sweeney, tell your old friend, Sweeney Todd—he'll cut their throats, too—he'll revenge you . . . Mistress Lovett. (*Kneeling beside body*) Mistress Lovett—answer me—speak to me, tell me who was the perpetrator of this foul crime. Why don't you answer? Ah, now—she's dead. Her tongue is silenced for ever. Are you burning down there in hell? (*Cradling the body in his arms like a child*) Don't cry Mistress Lovett, never mind—never mind, cry baby—never mind, Mistress Lovett. Are you weeping because you think you have missed your share, eh? Eh, is that it? (*puts down body*). You shall have your share alright, you shall have it to the last farthing. Look, my dear, I'll count it at your feet. (*Fetches cash box and starts to throw coins at her feet*) There—one sovereign, two, three, four, five, six.

Enter MARK.

Mark (*quietly*): Your trade was a paying one, Mr Todd.

Todd (*screams*): Go away! Go away! You're dead. Have you returned once more to haunt your murderer? I'll repent my sins, I'll give myself to the officers, only spare me the vision of your living corpse—spare me I say. (*On his knees*) I can bear no more of this. Take away this dreadful nightmare. Shall I never find rest again—never until I am as dead as this woman here and this man who stands before me now?

Mark (*moves to* TODD *and pulls him to his feet*): No, not dead, Mr Todd, not quite dead yet.

TODD *brings out a pistol from beneath his coat.*

Todd: Well, Mr Sailor, Sweeney Todd has never been known to miss yet; you'll be quite dead this time. (*Raises pistol to shoot*).

Smith (*springing out from a dark corner*): Not this time, Sweeney, not this time. (*Knocks pistol out of* TODD'S *hand as it goes off*).

Mark : Now, Mr Todd, it's your turn to sing low. With my own hands I shall drag you to the gallows and the end you so richly deserve.

Todd (*crouching in a corner behind a barrel*) : So, Mr Smith, so your tricks with the mechanism were of avail. You are both alive. Very well—the fortune of war. Take me alive if you can. (*Runs to back of stage and hides behind another barrel*).

Mark : Come from behind there, you villain! (*Advances towards* TODD *who rushes from barrel towards another*).

Todd : You'll never take me, I'll see you both in hell first! (*Turns over barrel which rolls towards* MARK *who in avoiding it fails to see* TODD *making for the down right door*).

Smith : There he goes—stop him. (*They chase after* TODD *who throws a large ladle at them which crashes at* SMITH'S *feet*).

Todd : I'll escape you yet. Observe! (*He has reached the door*) See, Mr Sailor, you are in my prison yet (*turns suddenly and runs through the door shouting as he goes*) You're fast now, all the doors are locked, one lever locks them all. You're fast now.

MARK *and* SMITH *run to the door and try to force it open in vain. They can hear* TODD'S *hoarse laugh as he mounts the stairs. They are shouting for help and hammering on the door as*

THE CURTAIN FALLS

ACT FOUR

SCENE THREE

TEMPLE STAIRS. *Enter* TOBIAS *and* JARVIS *from left, running.*

Tobias: Stay but a minute, kind Jarvis, for I must rest. Heaven knows the miles we've run in chase of that same villain who had me committed to that vile place from whence you rescued me.

Jarvis: But a moment then, for I am just as wishful to apprehend this murderer as you yourself. (*Sits on bench beside* TOBIAS).

Tobias: How was it that we came to lose the scent when we were in such close pursuit?

Jarvis: In truth I'm not at all sure how he did give us the slip, for once I swear I could have touched him if my legs could have taken me with greater speed. 'Twas in that marsh beyond the river that I nearly had him in my clutches, but the devil obtained a surer piece of ground than that which we trod upon and so were his footsteps hastened and he did reach the road and disappear from out of our view before we, too, were on the firmer soil.

Tobias: Supposing that he has returned to his barber's shop in Fleet Street. They do say that villains cannot restrain from revisiting the place where they carried out their dreadful crimes.

Jarvis: Do you believe him to be so much a fool? With half the officers of London on his heels the very last place he would wish to visit is that where he would be most widely known.

Tobias: As you say, kind Jarvis, it was but a foolish thought. Where then shall we go if we are to find this fiend and bring him to his final judgment?

Jarvis (*rising*): Perhaps you speak more sensibly than I at first perceived. Knowing that we and others like us would not expect him to return to his own lair, why should he not decide to try a cunning piece of bluff and go there hiding behind our disbelief of such a scheme to obtain his ill-gotten gains to sell for funds to finance himself whilst on the run.

Tobias: 'Tis worth our while to try. (*Rising*) Come, I am rested now and cannot wait to get once more into the chase of this inhuman brute.

Jarvis: Away then to the barber's shop in Fleet Street and our hope for meeting with its dreadful owner and the settlement of our account!

They run off right.

CURTAIN

ACT FOUR

SCENE FOUR

SWEENEY TODD'S SHOP

Todd (*searching furiously*) : Where are the jewels ? Was it here I hid them ?—or there ?—or there ? No—lost—forgotten! I will sit quietly and I will remember soon. (*Sits on chair left with his head resting on his hands.*)

Enter SIR WILLIAM BRANDON *in his judge's robes from door right. He stands in front of* TODD, *who starts up when he sees him.*

Judge : Good day to you, Mr Barber. I would like a shave and a quick one if you don't mind. I have to go and try a case at half past three.

Todd : But, sir, I much regret I cannot attend to you now.

Judge : And why not, pray ?

Todd : You see the shop is not open for custom at this hour.

Judge (*sternly!*) : Never mind; the door was open. Give me a shave, I say!

Todd : If you so insist, sir. P-p-pray sit down, sir. N-n-no, this one, sir (*indicates centre chair*). And I'll soon polish you off.

Judge : I beg your pardon, I am very short sighted. I cannot see your face properly but haven't I heard your voice before ?

Todd : I think you must be mistaken, sir. (*Puts towel around* JUDGE'S *neck*).

Judge : No mistake I assure you—since my eyes began to fail me I have come to rely more heavily on my ears to assist me with my memory.

Todd : Ah, sir, I have it now, I was once a foreman on the jury, sir.

Judge : Ah, that must have been it.

Todd : Excuse me, sir, for one moment—some hot water from the other room. Do not fear, however, I shall polish you off in no time at all—no time at all!

Exit TODD *through door up right.*

Todd (*returning into room*) : Polished him off!

But for some reason the chair has remained stationary and the JUDGE *still sits there.*

Todd (*not seeing the* JUDGE *and continuing with his search*) : I think I remember now. They were in the other room under a loose plank.

Judge (*testily*) : Barber, barber—what about my shave ? Am I to sit here all night ?

Todd (*starts*): I beg your p-p-pardon, sir, I am a little absent-minded this afternoon (*hurries out*).

Judge : Get on with it man, get on with it!

As he speaks the chair turns over and returns a moment or two later—empty. TODD *returns and continues with his search.*

Todd (*frantically pulling out drawers and looking behind cupboards*): There were other necklaces as well—some garnets I seem to remember. Oh, my head, my head! (*a knocking from up left*). Ah, knock away—knock away! My doors are as strong as the Bank of England. You should know, Mr Smith, for 'twas you that made them and in so doing made your own tomb. Ha, I had forgotten again—I must lock the door.

He goes to the door down right as it is thrown open by JARVIS *and* TOBIAS.

Jarvis : Here he is, Tobias—here he is! We were right. The villain returns to the scene of his many crimes. St George for England! (*Rushes at him.* TODD *flings him aside and rushes upstage left but the sound of thunderous knocking comes from below*).

Todd : Trapped! Trapped! (*flings himself on* JARVIS *but is flung to the ground*).

Jarvis : Hang on, Tobias, one foot apiece, hang on (*gradually they overpower him*). To the chair, Tobias, to the chair. As Shakespeare says, we'll hoist him with his own petard. (*They force* TODD *into the chair and* JARVIS *holds him there. The knocking from below is redoubled*).

Jarvis : Now, Tobias, the lever—you know where it is.

Tobias : No, no, Jarvis, 'twould be murder and we should all be hanged.

Jarvis : Out then—I'll do it myself (*rushes off up right*).

Knocking louder.

Enter JOHANNA, MR OAKLEY *and* LUPIN *from down right, running, followed closely by* PARMINE.

Parmine : Here he is, here in his own shop! Todd the murderer!

Enter SMITH *and* MARK *from upstage left.*

All : Mark Ingestre—alive!

Mark : Yes, Mark Ingestre, who, preserved from death by a miracle, returns to confound the guilty and protect the innocent. (JOHANNA *throws herself into his arms*).

Johanna : Mark, my own, my beloved, together again at last!

TODD *breaks from* TOBIAS's *hold and rushes to the cupboard where he obtains a razor.*

Tobias : Stop him, don't let him get away! (*All but* JOHANNA *close on* TODD *who sees them coming and brandishes the razor*).

Todd : You'll not have me. I'll escape you yet! (*Draws the razor across his throat and with blood gushing from his throat staggers to the centre chair into which he collapses. Slowly the chair begins to turn over and with a scream* TODD *disappears from view*).

JARVIS *runs back into the room and rushes to* TOBIAS.

Tobias : Free—free at last!

Johanna : Mark! (*She runs to* MARK *and he takes her in his arms to comfort her*).

Mark (*tenderly*) : Shed no more tears, Johanna, my own true love. We are reunited never to be parted again. Never more will we have cause to fear. The foul murderer Todd is dead and villainy has earned its just reward.

The whole company move downstage, face the audience and sing:

WHERE HAVE YOU GONE (Reprise)
(ENSEMBLE)

All :
Where has he gone, where is he now?
He's parted this earthly life.
Where has he gone, where is is now?
He's left all this mortal strife.
In London Town there's never been
A demon as black as 'he'
And sure to tell, down there in hell - - - - -

They all point down and move to the sides of the stage as the stage lights black out completely and a green light comes up on the centre chair in which TODD *is seated.*

Todd (*sings*): There's no one as evil as me!

Snap blackout.

CURTAIN

PRODUCTION NOTES

SETTINGS

Illustrations of the six main settings are given facing page 33. It is advisable to play the other scenes in front of traverse curtains to facilitate changes.

The basic set is the interior of Sweeney Todd's shop with the 'tipping' chair set upstage centre. This is a permanent structure and all other settings are placed downstage of this with the chair tipped back.

The chair is mounted on a light base identical in size with the flat against which it stands and to which it is fastened. When this is hinged to the stage floor, the chair can be tipped backwards so that the base fills the gap previously occupied by the back flat and the chair and its occupant are hidden from the audience. This is very simple to construct and most effective.

The other main settings can be either drop cloths or flats masked on either side by traverse curtains.

If the back flat for the court scene can be a gauze the effect of the apparition is heightened.

CASTING

When there is difficulty in obtaining a cast for this play the parts of the bystanders may be reduced or omitted and other parts doubled to enable the play to be performed by seven men and seven women.

It is intended that the part of Tobias be played by a girl particularly if the songs are used as these were written for a treble voice.

MUSIC

This version may be performed without the songs if required but they are very simple and were written for a cast with little experience of singing. Music must be used for background effect at various points in the play in keeping with the tradition of melodrama. The full piano score includes special background music composed for the play. This is obtainable on on hire from the publishers. A complete music plot appears on pages 93—94 and the melodies of the songs on pages 95—98.

If it is decided to omit the songs the play will end immediately before the final chorus.

PROPERTIES AND FURNITURE

A full list of the properties appears on pages 91—98. Furniture is best kept to a minimum; in fact the production at the Crescent Theatre used only two tables, three chairs, two benches and a stool.

LIGHTING

A full lighting plot appears on pages 89—90. No attempt should be made to make the lighting too realistic. The original play was performed when gas lighting was a novelty and the use of coloured glasses for special effects much in vogue. It is possible to heighten the play considerably by generous use of red acting area floods, green spots, etc., for creating atmosphere.

COSTUME AND MAKE-UP

This version is set in the early Victorian period and costume presents little problem. Make-up should be bold and with a tendency towards caricature. A bottle of theatrical blood is most important.

STYLE OF PERFORMANCE

This must be decided by the producer but it should be remembered that audiences at this type of play laugh more readily at overplaying than at burlesque. Audience participation is essential and should be encouraged in every possible way.

LIGHTING PLOT

ACT I — SCENE I

To open: Blackout
Cue 1: As clock strikes bring up spot covering graveyard only
Cue 2: On last stroke of clock bring up main lighting
Cue 3: End of reprise of "Sweeney Todd the Barber"—start slow fade of all except graveyard area
Cue 4: As Smith goes through gravestone 'door'—fade to blackout

ACT I — SCENE II

To open: Gloomy lighting with brighter pools on c. chair and d.s.c. and d.s.r. areas
Cue 5: Todd: . . . 'now that its master is sitting in it'—start slow fade blackout

ACT I — SCENE III

To open: Daylight interior
Cue 6: As Lupin goes off pursued by members of household—fade to blackout

ACT II — SCENE I

To open: Blackout, fading in at once to gloomy interior
Cue 7: Mrs Lovett: 'Oh, Lupy!—Lupy!' slow fade to blackout

ACT II — SCENE II

To open: As Act 1,— Scene 2
Cue 8: Exit of Lupin—fade to blackout, bring up green spot covering c. chair
Cue 9: Mark's rise from chair—fade out green spot and cross fade in main lighting at one third
Cue 10: As chair tips back with Mark—snap blackout
Cue 11: Entrance Todd—slight backing for practical lamp
Cue 12: End of "I'm Evil"—bring up main lighting
Cue 13: Todd: . . . 'holding hands like lovers'—slow fade to blackout

ACT II — SCENE III

To open: Main lighting
Cue 14: As Mrs Lovett raises trap door—quick fade to blackout

ACT II — SCENE IV

To open: Gloomy interior
Cue 15: Todd: . . . 'There is blood on my hands'—bring up red area flood, take out main lighting

ACT III — SCENE I

To open: As Act I, Scene II
Cue 16: Todd: . . . 'pronounced your doom'—take down main lighting to half
Cue 17: Todd lifts razor to cut Tobias's throat—main lighting to quarter, green spot on c. chair
Cue 18: Todd: . . . 'let me hence or it will kill me—ha! ha! ha!'—fade to blackout

ACT III — SCENE II

To open: Gloomy interior, shaft of sunlight from l. to light c. stage
Cue 19: Last line of reprise of "Heaven"—lighting full up

ACT III — SCENE III

To open: Moonlit exterior
Cue 20: Lupin's exit—snap blackout

ACT III — SCENE IV

To open: Main lighting interior, light behind gauze off
Cue 21: First appearance of Mark—main lighting to half, gauze light (green) on
Cue 22: Todd: . . . 'gleaming upon me from yonder window'—gauze light off, main up
Cue 23: Second appearance of Mark—main lighting to half, red spot on judge's box
Cue 24: Todd: . . . 'blood! blood! blood! Ha! ha! ha!'—spot out, main up
Cue 25: Todd: . . . 'and barter their eternal salvation'—main out, green spot on witness box
Cue 26: Todd: . . . 'a murderer! a murderer!'—fade to blackout

ACT IV — SCENE I

To open: Exterior daylight
Cue 27: As Lupin exit with bottle—fade to blackout

ACT IV — SCENE II

To open: Very dim interior, green flood on d.s.r. barrel area
Cue 28: Entrance of Mark—main lighting out, leave green flood on
Cue 29: As Smith and Mark call for help—fade to blackout

ACT IV — SCENE III

To open: Exterior—daylight
No Cues

ACT IV — SCENE IV

To open: Main lighting at two-thirds
Cue 30: Entrance of Mark and Smith—main lighting up
Cue 31: After penultimate line of reprise of "Where Have You Gone?"—snap blackout, green spot on c. chair to coincide
Cue 32: End of song—snap blackout

PROPERTY PLOT

ACT I — SCENE I

Personal: TODD: Razor
SMITH: Account

ACT I — SCENE II

On stage: Newspaper
Two shaving bibs
Razors
Comb
Hairbrush
Shaving brush
Shaving mug with ready mixed lather
Shaving soap

Personal: TODD: Razor, loaded blank cartridge pistol
MARK: Pearls in casket
PARMINE: Jeweller's glass

ACT I — SCENE III

On stage: Tablecloth
Miniature in frame

Personal: LUPIN: Brandy flask
JEFFREY: White rose
MEMBERS OF HOUSEHOLD: Shovel, tongs, mop, broom, frying pan

ACT II — SCENE I

On stage: Kettle
Teapot with tea
Two cups and saucers
Milk jug with milk
Stone rum bottle with liquid

Off stage: Pie on plate
Knife and fork
Napkin

Personal: MRS LOVETT: Knitting
LUPIN: Umbrella

ACT II — SCENE II

On stage: As Act I — Scene II

Personal: TODD: Lamp (practical)

ACT II — SCENE III

On stage: Trays of pies on counter

Personal: JARVIS: Silver toothpick

ACT II — SCENE IV

On stage: Three barrels
Trays of pies (two to be eaten)

Personal: PARMINE: Iron bar
TODD: Small account book
MRS LOVETT: Dagger

ACT III — SCENE I

On stage: As Act I — Scene II
Personal: TODD : Casket with pearls, razor

ACT III — SCENE II

On stage: Ledger
Large handbell
Ink pot
Quill Pen
Large bunch of keys
Personal: TODD : Walking stick

ACT III — SCENE III

On stage: Nil
Personal: TODD : String of pearls

ACT III — SCENE IV

On stage: Letter
Gavel
Personal: USHER : Pearls in casket

ACT IV — SCENE I

On stage: Pewter tankards
Three stone bottles
Personal: WARDERS : Keys, staves

ACT IV — SCENE II

On stage: Three barrels
Cash box with sovereigns
Personal: TODD : Loaded blank cartridge pistol

ACT IV — SCENE III

Nil

ACT IV — SCENE IV

On stage: As Act I — Scene II
Personal: TODD : Razor

MUSIC PLOT

OVERTURE

ACT I — SCENE I

1. 'Sweeney Todd the Barber'. (*Song:* TODD)
2. 'Sailing Away'. (*Song:* TOBIAS)
3. B minor chord. (MARK: '. . . . *the possessor of a string of pearls*')
4. 'Sweeney Todd the Barber'. (*Reprise of Song*)
5. Link music—S.T.T.B. chorus only

ACT I — SCENE II

6. B minor chord (*as chair tips back*)
7. B minor chord (*as chair returns*)
8. B minor chord (*as chair tips back*)
9. B minor chord (*as chair returns*)
10. Link music—S.T.T.B. in G minor and verse 'Where Have You Gone ?'

ACT I — SCENE III

11. 'Where Have You Gone ?' (*Song:* JOHANNA)
12. 'I'm the Master'. (*Song:* JASPER)
13. 'Where Have You Gone ?' (*Music of chorus only:* JOHANNA: '*I cannot tell what . . .*')
14. 'I'm the Master (music). (*Chase at end of scene*)
15. Link music—'Verily, Verily, So'

ACT II — SCENE I

16. 'Verily, Verily, So'. (*Song:* LUPIN)
17. Link music—'Verily, Verily, So' and S.T.T.B. in G minor

ACT II — SCENE II

18. S.T.T.B. in G minor—chorus only. (TODD *chasing* LUPIN)
19. B minor chord (broken) (*as chair tips back*)
20. B minor chord (broken) (*as chair tips forward*)
21. C minor chord (*as chair tips back*) leading into :
22. 'I'm Evil'. (*Song:* TODD)
23. 'Dear Mistress L.' (*Song:* TODD and MRS LOVETT)
24. Link music—'Dear Mistress L.'

ACT II — SCENE III

25. Link music—B minor chords

ACT II — SCENE IV

26. B minor chord (broken). (PARMINE : ' . . . *in this disgusting speculation*')
27. B minor chord (broken). (TODD's *entrance*)
28. 'Where Have You Gone ?' (Music of chorus only : MRS LOVETT : ' . . . *good lady and gentleman*')
29. Chromatic music based on B minor. (TODD : '*There is blood on my hands*')

INTERVAL

ACT III — SCENE I

30. Opening music—chorus of 'Heaven'
31. 'It's My Mother's Birthday'. (*Song:* TOBIAS)
32. 'It's My Mother's Birthday' (music of chorus). (TODD : '*... eh, do you remember it ?*')
33. S.T.T.B. in G minor. (*Chase of* TOBIAS *and* TODD)
34. Discord—(*as chair tips forward*)
35. Link music—S.T.T.B. in G minor and 'Heaven'

ACT III — SCENE II

36. S.T.T.B. in G minor. (*To open*)
37. 'Heaven'. (*Song:* TOBIAS)
38. F minor chords (*Fight*) leading into :
39. 'Heaven'. (*Reprise of song:* TOBIAS *and* JARVIS)
40. Link music—'Heaven' and 'Where Have You Gone ?'

ACT III — SCENE III

41. B minor chord (broken). (*Entrance of* TODD)
42. B minor chord (broken) plus chromatic music. (TODD : '*... follow me*')
43. B minor chord (broken). (TODD : '*... an undeniable one*')
44. B minor chord (broken) plus chromatic music. (*Exit of* TODD)
45. 'Verily, Verily, So'. (*End of scene*)

ACT III — SCENE IV

46. S.T.T.B. in G minor. (*End of scene*)
47. Link music—'Here In The Jug'

ACT IV — SCENE I

48. 'Here In The Jug'. (*Song:* CHORUS)
49. B minor chord (broken). (1ST WARDER : *... The bird has flown*')
50. 'Verily, Verily, So' (music). (LUPIN : '*... crying sins of this nation*')
51. Link music—'Verily, Verily, So' and S.T.T.B. in G minor

ACT IV — SCENE II

52. S.T.T.B. in G minor. (TODD : '*... I'll escape you yet*')
53. Link music—'I'm Evil'

ACT IV — SCENE III

54. S.T.T.B. in G minor. (*End of scene*)
55. Link music—'I'm Evil'

ACT IV — SCENE IV

56. B minor chord (broken) (*as chair tips back*)
57. B minor chord (broken) (*as chair returns*)
58. B minor chord (broken) (*as chair tips back*)
59. 'Where Have You Gone ?' (*Reprise of chorus of song:* ENSEMBLE)
60. Heaven (during CURTAIN CALL)

Sweeney Todd The Barber

Sailing Away

Where Have You Gone?

I'm the Master

Verily, Verily So

I'm Evil

Dear Mistress L.

My Mother's Birthday

Heaven

Here in the Jug

PRODUCER'S NOTES

LIGHTING NOTES